Church of Scotland

Prayers for Family Worship

Church of Scotland

Prayers for Family Worship

ISBN/EAN: 9783337291488

Printed in Europe, USA, Canada, Australia, Japan

Cover: Foto ©Lupo / pixelio.de

More available books at **www.hansebooks.com**

Aids to Devotion

PRAYERS

FOR

FAMILY WORSHIP

AUTHORISED BY THE

General Assembly of the Church of Scotland

WILLIAM BLACKWOOD AND SONS
EDINBURGH AND LONDON
MDCCCXCII

PREFACE.

The Church of Scotland has always sought to encourage the practice of family worship, believing it to be essential to family godliness and growth in grace; and the General Assembly has frequently authorised the publication of prayers for the use of those who wish to conduct family worship with such aid.

The 'Aids to Devotion' published on previous occasions have met with great acceptance, and this volume is issued in the hope that, by the blessing of God, it may help to foster healthy and joyous spiritual life in many Christian families. It is the result of careful revision of earlier books. The prayers have been rearranged and shortened. Many passages from the writings of devout men, who have been leaders of thought in all the different ages of the Christian Church, have been incorporated to give variety of expression, and to excite and maintain devotional feeling.

The book contains morning and evening prayers for four weeks. Besides general supplications and intercessions, each prayer includes a reference to a special subject, which is indicated in the Index. There are also prayers for Sacramental occasions, and a service for the sick, with special prayers for use in the sick-room.

The General Assembly of 1892 approved of this volume of prayers, and authorised its publication.

By Authority of the General Assembly's Committee on 'Aids to Devotion.'

JOHN PATON, *Convener.*

CONTENTS.

PRAYERS FOR FAMILY WORSHIP.

First Week.

	PAGE
Lord's Day Morning...For grace to use holy ordinances,	13
Lord's Day Evening....Thanksgiving for holy ordinances,	15
Monday Morning........For guidance during the week,	18
Monday Evening........For Divine Fatherly blessings,	20
Tuesday Morning.......For Divine blessing during the day,	23
Tuesday Evening........For Divine protection during the night,	25
Wednesday Morning...Thanksgiving,	27
Wednesday Evening....For a sense of Divine goodness,	30
Thursday Morning.....For mercy, and grace to serve God,	32
Thursday Evening......For pardon, and power to obey,	34
Friday Morning.........For Divine guidance in daily work,	37
Friday Evening..........For steadfastness in holy things,	40
Saturday Morning......For sanctification,	42
Saturday Evening.......For preparation for heaven,	44

Second Week.

Lord's Day Morning...General confession and supplication,	48
Lord's Day Evening....For power to grow in grace,	51
Monday Morning........For God's continual help,	53
Monday Evening........For power to trust in God,	56

Tuesday Morning........	For temporal mercies, . .	58
Tuesday Evening........	For contentment, ...	60
Wednesday Morning...	For faith in Christ, . .	63
Wednesday Evening....	For grace to love God, . . .	65
Thursday Morning......	For power to overcome sin, .	67
Thursday Evening......	For the gift of the Spirit, . .	70
Friday Morning.........	For Divine help and guidance, .	72
Friday Evening..........	For Divine pardon and guardianship,	74
Saturday Morning......	For grace to love our brethren, .	77
Saturday Evening.......	For power to persevere, . . .	79

Third Week.

Lord's Day Morning...	Thanksgiving for ordinances, . .	82
Lord's Day Evening....	For grace to use God's word, . .	84
Monday Morning........	For power to serve God in daily life,	87
Monday Evening........	For pardon, and power to repent, .	89
Tuesday Morning.......	For faith, ...	91
Tuesday Evening........	For hope, ...	93
Wednesday Morning...	For charity, ...	95
Wednesday Evening....	For spiritual peace, . . .	98
Thursday Morning......	For grace to imitate Christ, . .	100
Thursday Evening	For power to exercise self-denial, .	102
Friday Morning.........	For temporal mercies, . . .	104
Friday Evening..........	Thanksgiving, ...	107
Saturday Morning......	For help to discharge our duty, .	109
Saturday Evening.......	For grace to seek for heavenly things,	111

Fourth Week.

Lord's Day Morning...	Praise, confession, and supplication,	114
Lord's Day Evening....	Thanksgiving and intercession, .	116
Monday Morning........	For grace to walk with God, . .	119
Monday Evening	For self-knowledge and watchfulness,	121
Tuesday Morning.......	For self-control, ...	123

Tuesday Evening........For power to trust in Providence, .	125
Wednesday Morning...For grace to be meek and gentle, .	127
Wednesday Evening...For power to love Christ, . .	130
Thursday Morning......For power to live a Christian life, .	132
Thursday Evening.........For grace to be patient and contented,	134
Friday Morning.........For help to be earnest in religious duty, ...	136
Friday Evening..........For grace to be humble, . . .	139
Saturday Morning......For enlightenment and confirmation in the Lord, ...	141
Saturday Evening.......For grace to prepare for death, .	144

PRAYERS FOR SACRAMENTAL OCCASIONS.

Morning Prayer in preparation for the Holy Communion,	149
Evening Prayer in preparation for the Holy Communion, .	152
For Morning of a Communion Sunday, ...	154
For Evening of a Communion Sunday, ...	157

SERVICE FOR THE SICK, ...	161

SPECIAL PRAYERS FOR USE IN THE SICK-ROOM.

For a sick child, ...	167
For one whose sickness has been long continued, . .	168
For one about to undergo a serious surgical operation, .	169
Prayer in case of sudden illness or accident, . . .	170
For a woman in travail, ...	171
Thanksgiving for deliverance in travail, ...	172
For one who is insensible or delirious, ...	173
For a sick person in deep dejection of spirit, . . .	174
For a sick person when there is little hope of recovery, .	175
For one at the point of death, ...	177

Prayers for Family Worship.

"They shall prosper that love Thee."—PSALM cxxii. 6.

"As for me and my house, we will serve the Lord."—JOSHUA xxiv. 15.

𝕺𝖚𝖗 𝕱𝖆𝖙𝖍𝖊𝖗 which art in heaven, Hallowed be Thy name. Thy kingdom come. Thy will be done in earth, as it is in heaven. Give us this day our daily bread. And forgive us our debts, as we forgive our debtors. And lead us not into temptation, but deliver us from evil: For Thine is the kingdom, and the power, and the glory, for ever.—𝔄𝔪𝔢𝔫.

FAMILY WORSHIP should begin by reading a portion of Scripture; and it is recommended that the Old Testament should be read in the morning, and the New Testament in the evening.

Prayers for Family Worship.

FIRST WEEK.

Lord's Day Morning.

"This is the day which the Lord hath made; we will rejoice and be glad in it."

LET US PRAY.

O GOD, who hast promised to be present with Thy people, and to grant their requests for whatsoever things they may ask of Thee in the name of Thy beloved Son, regard us, we beseech Thee, with Thy favour, and graciously fulfil Thy promise in our behalf; that, offering up our desires unto Thee for things agreeable to Thy most blessed will, we may obtain the petitions that we ask of Thee, through Jesus Christ our Lord.

Direct our thoughts to those things which belong to Thy glory and to our own everlasting peace.

We bless Thee for the spiritual privileges which have been secured to us in Jesus Christ our Lord; for our peaceful Sabbaths; for the holy sacraments; for Thy revealing to us in Thy Word all which it is necessary for us to know, believe, and practise for our eternal salvation; for our consolation under the ills of life, and for our hopes of a heavenly inheritance beyond death and the grave.

Pardon, O God, our past neglect of Thine ordinances; and now that thou callest us to remember the Sabbath-day and keep it holy, we humbly implore the aid of Thy Spirit.

Prepare our hearts for Thy service, and enable us to rest this day from all our works, as Thou didst from Thine.

O God, who hast promised that in all places where Thou dost record Thy name Thou wilt come unto Thy people and bless them, vouchsafe to us, and to our fellow-worshippers in every place, Thy presence and blessing. Guide Thy ministering servants in all the offices of Thy worship, and enable them faithfully to declare the truths of Thy Gospel. And grant that their ministrations may be effectual for the conversion of sinners, and for the building up of saints in holiness and comfort through faith unto salvation.

Be very gracious to those who are withheld by sickness, or any other necessary cause, from worshipping Thee in the assemblies of Thy people.

Have pity on those who wilfully forsake Thine ordinances and profane Thy holy day.

Increase everywhere the number of Thy true worshippers; and hasten the time when, in every place, incense shall be offered unto Thy name, and a pure offering.

To Thy special care and guidance we this day commit ourselves, and all who are dear to us. O send out Thy light and Thy truth: let them lead us; let them bring us unto Thy holy hill and to Thy tabernacles.

Graciously hear us, for the sake of Thy beloved Son, to whom, with Thee and with the Holy Spirit, be glory and majesty, dominion and blessing, world without end.

OUR Father which art in heaven, Hallowed be Thy name. Thy kingdom come. Thy will be done in earth, as it is in heaven. Give us this day our daily bread. And forgive us our debts, as we forgive our debtors. And lead us not into temptation, but deliver us from evil: For Thine is the kingdom, and the power, and the glory, for ever.—*Amen.*

Lord's Day Evening.

"O Lord, I cry unto Thee: make haste unto me; give ear unto my voice, when I cry unto Thee.

"Let my prayer be set forth before Thee as incense, and the lifting up of my hands as the evening sacrifice."

Let us Pray.

ALMIGHTY GOD, Father of lights, from whom cometh down every good and perfect gift, we lift up our souls unto Thee.

We thank Thee for the instructions of Thy Word, the rest of Thy Sabbath, the ordinances of Thy worship, and all our Christian privileges and means of grace; and for the promise of Thy Holy Spirit to bless them, and make them effectual for our salvation.

Make us duly sensible, we beseech Thee, of the great and manifold privileges Thou hast conferred upon us. Enter not into judgment with us Thy servants for our faithlessness and neglect.

Teach us that, denying ungodliness and worldly lusts, we should live soberly, righteously, and godly in this present world, looking for that blessed hope, and the glorious appearing of the great God and our Saviour Jesus Christ.

Almighty God, who hast called us with a holy calling, perfect that which is lacking in our faith, and make us to increase in love to Thee and to our fellowmen.

O Lord our God, who hast graciously promised an everlasting rest to Thy people hereafter, and hast given Thy Sabbath to foreshadow it, and to prepare us for it; let us therefore fear lest a promise being left us of entering into Thy rest, any of us should seem to come short of it.

We pray that here and everywhere Thy Word may have free course and may be glorified; that Thy ministering servants may be faithful, and Thy people fruitful in every good work; that Thy Church may be edified, purified, and extended; that the outcasts of Israel and the fulness of the Gentiles may be gathered into the fold of the great Shepherd and Bishop of souls; and that the blessed day may soon come when the knowledge of Thy Gospel shall cover the whole earth.

We pray for the welfare of our Sovereign; for the good of our country; and for the peace of all nations.

Remember the sick, the dying, and all who are in danger or distress. Comfort and support them, and give them a happy issue out of all their troubles.

Regard with Thy favour all the members of this household, and enable us, by all good fidelity in our appointed stations, to honour and serve Thee our Master in heaven.

[Bestow Thy blessing on the children of this family. Guide them in ways of holiness; and satisfy them early with Thy mercy, that they may rejoice and be glad all their days.]

To Thy fatherly care, O God, we commend ourselves and all who are dear to us. Inasmuch as Thou hast appointed the night for rest and the day for labour, lighten our darkness, we beseech Thee, O God, and by Thy great mercy defend us from all perils of this night. Sanctify the rest of the same to us, that we may be made fitter for the labours of the next day; and so both day and night being spent according to Thy will, we may be prepared for that great day of Thine, which hath no night succeeding. Grant this, O God, for the sake of Thine only Son our Saviour, to whom, with Thee and with the Holy Spirit, be honour and praise for ever and ever.

OUR Father which art in heaven, Hallowed be Thy name. Thy kingdom come. Thy will be done in earth, as it is in heaven. Give us this day our daily bread. And forgive us our debts, as we forgive our debtors. And lead us not into temptation, but deliver us from evil: For Thine is the kingdom, and the power, and the glory, for ever.—*Amen.*

Monday Morning.

"It is of the Lord's mercies that we are not consumed, because His compassions fail not. They are new every morning."

Let us Pray.

O GOD, our Creator and Preserver, who, by the rest of Thy holy Sabbath, and by the sleep of the past night, hast restored our souls and refreshed our bodies, we thankfully acknowledge Thy goodness, and yield ourselves anew to Thy service.

Suffer us not, we beseech Thee, when returning to our daily work, to forget the instructions of Thy Word, or to lose the hallowed influence of Thy worship. Help us to carry the spirit of the Sabbath into the business of the week, so that, amidst all our labours, our souls may still rest in Thee, and whether we eat or drink, or whatsoever we do, we may do all to Thy glory.

We confess, O God, that our goodness has often been as a morning cloud or the early dew, that passeth away. Pardon our unsteadfastness, and give us grace that we may be enabled constantly to walk with Thee. Let the life we henceforth lead be a life of faith in the Son of God, who loved us and gave Himself for us.

O Lord, without whom we can do nothing as we ought, help us in all our actions to take heed unto Thy Word, and to abstain from every form of evil. Set a watch before our mouths, and keep the door of our lips, that no corrupt communications may proceed from them. Cleanse our hearts from unholy desires and uncharitable dispositions, and enable us so to manifest the power of godliness, that we may be epistles of Christ, known and read of all men.

Grant us this day Thy guidance and protection. Aid us in our appointed occupations. Deliver us from all infirmities of temper. Guide us in business. Support us in any trials or dangers that may befall us. Help us to endure as seeing Thee who art invisible; and while we are diligent in seeking the things that are needful for this present world, may it be our chief concern to lay up treasure in heaven.

Let Thy blessing rest on the inmates of this dwelling. Give grace to all of us to discharge our several duties, as parents or children, masters or servants, with uprightness, fidelity, and diligence.

Bestow Thy favour on our relatives and friends. Prosper all the interests of our country. Bless our Sovereign, and all in authority over us, and dispose them ever to rule in Thy fear.

Provide for the poor. Instruct the ignorant. Reclaim the erring. Pity the afflicted. Impart relief and comfort to the sick, and prepare for their great change those who are about to die.

We pray for all our brethren of mankind, that it may please Thee to diffuse among them the knowledge of Thy truth, and to bring them to the faith and obedience of Thy Gospel.

Graciously hear our supplications, for the sake of Thy beloved Son, our Lord and Saviour, who taught us in our prayers to say thus:—

Our Father which art in heaven, Hallowed be Thy name. Thy kingdom come. Thy will be done in earth, as it is in heaven. Give us this day our daily bread. And forgive us our debts, as we forgive our debtors. And lead us not into temptation, but deliver us from evil: For Thine is the kingdom, and the power, and the glory, for ever.—*Amen.*

Monday Evening.

"Give ear unto my prayer, O God; and hide not Thyself from my supplication. I will call upon God; and the Lord shall save me. Evening, morning, and at noon, will I pray, and cry aloud; and He shall hear my voice."

LET US PRAY.

ALMIGHTY GOD, Father of our Lord Jesus Christ, give us, we beseech Thee, the spirit of adoption, while we pour out before Thee the desires of our hearts. Grant that, coming unto Thee with holy reverence and confidence, as children to a Father able and ready to help us, we may be accepted in the name of Thy beloved Son, and through Him receive the petitions which we ask of Thee.

Holy Father, we are not worthy to be called Thy children. We confess that we have been unthankful for Thy mercies, distrustful of Thy promises, and disobedient to Thy commandments. We have despised Thy fatherly chastenings. We have set at nought Thy counsel, and would none of Thy reproof. We have kept back from Thee the affection of our hearts, and by our manifold wickedness have provoked Thee to cast us off.

Merciful Father, grant us Thy forgiveness. Work in us true repentance towards Thee, and faith unfeigned towards the Lord Jesus Christ; and for His sake be merciful to our unrighteousness, and remember our iniquities no more.

Give unto us also Thy Holy Spirit, to witness with our spirits that we are Thy children. Make us kindly affectioned to our brethren, ready to bear with their infirmities, and to do them good as we have opportunity. Amidst the toils and trials of our present condition, support and comfort us with the hope of the heavenly inheritance.

O Thou bountiful Giver of all good, who knowest what things we have need of before we ask, we cast ourselves on Thy care, and plead with Thee, according to Thy promises, for all things needful or expedient for us. Grant us, in all our duties, Thy help; in all our difficulties, Thy counsel; in all our dangers, Thy protection; in all our troubles, Thy peace. And whatsoever it may please Thee to give or to withhold, teach us to trust in Thine assurance that all things work together for good to them that love Thee, and to rest contented with Thy will.

Father of mercies, whose power hath sustained us, whose bounty hath provided for us, whose love hath redeemed us, we render praise and thanksgiving unto Thee, acknowledging that we are not worthy of the least of all Thy benefits; and we beseech Thee so to impress them on our hearts, that we may show our thankfulness by a cheerful and steadfast obedience to Thy commandments.

We pray for all our relatives and friends, that they may be blessed with Thy favour and protection. Forgive our enemies, and reward our benefactors. We pray for those who are in affliction, that it may please Thee to comfort and relieve them.

Look with compassion on the whole human race. Promote their peace, liberty, and happiness; and above all, bring them to the knowledge of Thy truth.

And now, O God, we commit ourselves to Thee. Grant us quiet sleep, and mercifully spare us to enjoy the blessings and discharge the duties of another day.

Graciously hear us, for the sake of Thy beloved Son, our Lord and Saviour.

OUR Father which art in heaven, Hallowed be Thy name. Thy kingdom come. Thy will be done in earth, as it is in heaven. Give us this day our daily bread. And forgive us our debts, as we forgive our debtors. And lead us not into temptation, but deliver us from evil: For Thine is the kingdom, and the power, and the glory, for ever.—*Amen.*

Tuesday Morning.

"Hearken unto the voice of my cry, my King and my God: for unto Thee will I pray. My voice shalt Thou hear in the morning, O Lord; in the morning will I direct my prayer unto Thee, and will look up."

LET US PRAY.

ALMIGHTY GOD, our Father and Preserver, we give Thee thanks that of Thy goodness Thou hast watched over us during the past night, and brought us to see the light of another day. Strengthen and guard us by Thy grace, we beseech Thee, that we may spend this day in Thy service, seeking Thy glory and the good of our fellow-men. Cause us to hear Thy loving-kindness in the morning, for in Thee do we trust. Cause us to know the way wherein we should walk; for we lift up our souls unto Thee.

We confess, O God, that by reason of our manifold sins we are unworthy to seek any blessing at Thy hands; but we beseech Thee, for the sake of Thy beloved Son, to blot out all our iniquities. Let them no longer come between us and Thee, hiding from us the light of Thy countenance; but of Thy boundless mercy be pleased to forgive them, and to remember them no more.

Help us for the time to come to yield ourselves entirely to Thy service. Let it be the purpose of our lives to honour Thee, and to do only such things as are pleasing in Thy sight.

Assist us in the duties of our calling. Grant that while we are not slothful in business, we may also be fervent in spirit, serving the Lord. And enable us, while labouring for the life that now is, to look ever beyond it to that heavenly life which Thou hast promised to Thy children.

Defend us, O God, in soul and body, from all evil. Guard us against the assaults of the devil, the snares of the world, and the sinful desires of our own hearts. Continue and increase Thy grace within us, until we be perfected in the glory of our Lord Jesus Christ.

We commend to Thy fatherly care all whom we should remember in prayer, asking Thee to pardon their sins, and to make them holy with the holiness of Christ, and to guide them by Thy Spirit.

Remember in Thy great mercy the poor, the suffering, and those appointed soon to die. Relieve and comfort and sustain them, O God, by Thy heavenly grace, and grant that finally they may rest with Thee.

Extend Thy compassion, we beseech Thee, to all mankind. Put an end to war, discord, vice, and superstition everywhere, and cause that all the nations may speedily be enlightened and sanctified by the Gospel of Jesus Christ.

Bless our native land. May the light of the Gospel of Jesus Christ be the glory thereof, and Thy fear our strength.

Graciously hear our humble supplications, according to the riches of Thy mercy in Jesus Christ, our Lord and only Saviour.

OUR Father which art in heaven, Hallowed be Thy name. Thy kingdom come. Thy will be done in earth, as it is in heaven. Give us this day our daily bread. And forgive us our debts, as we forgive our debtors. And lead us not into temptation, but deliver us from evil: For Thine is the kingdom, and the power, and the glory, for ever.—*Amen.*

Tuesday Evening.

"As for me and my house, we will serve the Lord."

Let us Pray.

O GOD, who hast appointed the night for rest and the day for labour, grant, we beseech Thee, that we may so rest in peace and quietness during the coming night, that afterwards we may be fitted for our appointed labours. Take us into Thy holy protection, so that no evil may befall us, and no plague come nigh our dwelling. Although we have not passed this day without greatly sinning against Thee, yet let it please Thee, for the sake of Thy beloved Son, to hide our sins with Thy mercy, as Thou coverest all things on earth with the darkness of the night, and to bury them evermore out of Thy remembrance; and grant that as our bodies are refreshed by quiet sleep, so also our minds may be made tranquil by a comfortable sense of Thy forgiveness.

We thank Thee, O God, that Thou hast not appointed us to wrath, but to obtain salvation by our Lord Jesus Christ, who died for us, that whether we wake or sleep, we should live together with Him. Help us, we pray Thee, with true faith to rest on Him, and all our life long with purpose of heart to cleave to Him. And when at length our days are ended and our work is finished in this world, grant that we may depart hence in the blessed comfort of Thy favour, and in the sure hope of that glorious kingdom where there is day without night, and life without the shadow of death, for ever.

We pray for Thy blessing on our beloved friends. Guard them from evil by night and by day. Supply their wants out of Thy glorious riches, and above all, enrich them with spiritual and heavenly blessings.

[Regard with Thy favour the children of this family. Deliver them from the temptations that surround them, and cause them to grow in knowledge and in grace.]

May all the members of this household, in their several places and relations, find their appointed toil dignified and sweetened to them by the thought that in all things they are serving the Lord Christ.

We implore Thy blessing for all widows and orphans; and for the poor, the sick, the sorrowful, and the dying. Succour and relieve them according to their necessities; and overrule Thy dealings with them for their spiritual good.

Bestow Thy favour on the British Empire and all its Colonies. Preserve to us our liberties and privileges. Bless our Sovereign and all in authority;

enable them to rule in Thy fear; and grant that under them all orders of the people may lead quiet and peaceable lives in all godliness and honesty.

O God, who hast made of one blood all nations, and wouldst have all men to come to the knowledge of the truth, open, we beseech Thee, a great door and effectual for the preaching of Thy blessed Gospel everywhere; and hasten the time when all the ends of the earth shall turn to Thee, and all the kindreds of the nations shall worship before Thee.

And now, O Lord our God, we entreat Thee, incline Thine ear to the voice of our supplications, which we present unto Thee in the name of Thy beloved Son, our Lord and Saviour, in whose words we further pray:—

Our Father which art in heaven, Hallowed be Thy name. Thy kingdom come. Thy will be done in earth, as it is in heaven. Give us this day our daily bread. And forgive us our debts, as we forgive our debtors. And lead us not into temptation, but deliver us from evil: For Thine is the kingdom, and the power, and the glory, for ever.—*Amen.*

Wednesday Morning.

"I will sing of Thy power; yea, I will sing aloud of Thy mercy in the morning: for Thou hast been my defence and refuge in the day of my trouble. Unto Thee, O my strength, will I sing: for God is my defence, and the God of my mercy."

Let us Pray.

ALMIGHTY and most merciful Father, it is a good thing to give thanks unto Thee, to sing praises unto Thy name, O Thou Most High, to show forth Thy loving-kindness in the morning, and Thy faithfulness every night.

We thank Thee for having created us after Thine own image, and endowed us with the gifts of reason and of conscience.

We thank Thee for the bounties of Thy providence; for health and strength; for food and raiment; for manifold social blessings and domestic comforts; for seasonable help in our times of need; for consolation in our hours of sorrow; and for all the care and kindness Thou hast shown to us from our birth even until now.

Above all, we magnify Thy name for Thine unspeakable mercy to our souls. We thank Thee that Thou hast given Thy beloved Son to be the propitiation for our sins; that Thou hast promised Thy Holy Spirit to sanctify our corrupt nature; that Thou hast called us out of darkness into the marvellous light of Thy Gospel; that Thou hast abundantly favoured us with means of grace, and hast comforted us with the hope of glory.

Have mercy on us, O God, after Thy loving-kindness; according to the multitude of Thy tender mercies, blot out our transgressions; and for the sake of Thy beloved Son, continue to us Thy love, and visit us with the joy of Thy salvation.

O God, by whose good hand upon us we have been

spared to see the light of another day, and in whose merciful providence we are now called to go forth to our work and labour until the evening, grant us, in all our occupations, the aid of Thy strength and the guidance of Thy wisdom. Teach us in all our ways to acknowledge Thee, and do Thou direct our steps. And whatsoever we do, in word or in deed, enable us to do all in the name of the Lord Jesus, giving thanks unto Thee, even our Father, by Him.

Graciously hear us, O God, while we plead with Thee for all whom we ought to remember at a throne of grace.

Bestow Thy favour on our kindred and friends. Reward with Thy bounty all that have done us good. Pardon all who have done or wished us evil, and enable us to forgive them from the heart.

God of all comfort, have pity on the afflicted. Send them Thy grace to sustain them in their hours of trial. And let Thy chastening, though for the present it seemeth grievous, yield in them afterward the peaceable fruit of righteousness.

Look with compassion on the whole world. Hasten the time when repentance and remission of sins shall be preached in the name of Jesus to all nations; and grant that wherever Thy Gospel is already known, its holy and blessed fruits may be more and more abundant.

Hear our prayers, O God, and accept our praises, for the sake of Thy beloved Son our Saviour, to whom, with Thee and the Holy Ghost, be ascribed all glory, thanksgiving, and dominion, world without end.

OUR Father which art in heaven, Hallowed be

Thy name. Thy kingdom come. Thy will be done in earth, as it is in heaven. Give us this day our daily bread. And forgive us our debts, as we forgive our debtors. And lead us not into temptation, but deliver us from evil: For Thine is the kingdom, and the power, and the glory, for ever.—*Amen.*

Wednesday Evening.

"In everything by prayer and supplication with thanksgiving let your requests be made known unto God."

LET US PRAY.

O GOD, who by Thy merciful providence hast upheld us throughout the past day, and under whose care we feel that we can lay ourselves down and sleep in peace during the coming night, we acknowledge our dependence on Thee, and lift up our souls in thanksgiving for Thy goodness.

Pardon, we beseech Thee, for the sake of Thy dear Son, our past ingratitude for Thy manifold lovingkindnesses. Remember no more against us our transgressions. Continue to us temporal and spiritual blessings, and teach us henceforth to show our thankfulness for them, by giving up ourselves to Thy service, and doing those things that are pleasing in Thy sight.

Grant, O God, that our experience of Thy goodness may lead us at all times to put our trust in Thee. Cause us to feel assured that Thou, who hast blessed us hitherto, wilt bless us still, and wilt withhold from us nothing which, in Thine unerring wisdom, Thou knowest to be needful or expedient for us.

Grant also that a due sense of Thine unmerited kindness may subdue in us every feeling of discontent. May we meekly submit to our hardships or deprivations, acknowledging that they are not worthy to be compared with the bounties of Thy providence and the riches of Thy grace.

Father of mercies, who art kind unto the unthankful and to the evil, teach us to be generous towards all men, to love our enemies, to bless them that curse us, and do good to them that hate us, to walk in love as Thou hast loved us, and from the heart to forgive one another, even as Thou for Christ's sake hast forgiven us.

God of all grace, we beseech Thee, have mercy on all our brethren of mankind, and bring them to the knowledge and reception of Thy truth. Grant that true religion, which exalteth a nation, may prevail more and more in our native land. By their holiness and good works may all the people praise Thee.

We pray for the sons and daughters of affliction, that it may please Thee to comfort and relieve them, and to overrule Thy fatherly chastening to their eternal good.

And now, O God, we commit ourselves to Thee. Watch over us during the darkness of the night. Save us from all dangers. Grant us refreshing sleep; and bring us in peace to the light of a new day.

Graciously hear us, O Father, and have mercy on us, for the sake of Thy beloved Son, our Strength and our Redeemer.

OUR Father which art in heaven, Hallowed be Thy name. Thy kingdom come. Thy will be done in earth, as it is in heaven. Give us this day our daily bread. And forgive us our debts, as we forgive our debtors. And lead us not into temptation, but deliver us from evil: For Thine is the kingdom, and the power, and the glory, for ever.—*Amen.*

Thursday Morning.

"Unto Thee, O Lord, do I lift up my soul. O my God, I trust in Thee.

"Show me Thy ways, O Lord; teach me Thy paths. Lead me in Thy truth, and teach me: for Thou art the God of my salvation; on Thee do I wait all the day."

Let us Pray.

ALMIGHTY GOD, our heavenly Father, who knowest what things we have need of before we ask, and art able to do exceeding abundantly above all that we ask or think, direct and aid us, we beseech Thee, in our supplications; that though of ourselves we know not how to pray, and are not worthy that Thou shouldst grant our requests, we may ask and obtain whatsoever is expedient for us, according to Thy glorious riches in Christ Jesus; to whom, with Thee and with the Holy Spirit, be honour and praise for evermore.

O God, who hast set our iniquities before Thee, and our secret sins in the light of Thy countenance, we humble ourselves in Thy most holy presence, acknowledging our utter unworthiness in Thy sight. We have cause to be ashamed before Thee, when we remember how little we have thought upon Thee; how often we have forgotten Thee; and how many have been our sins against our fellow-men.

Enter not, O Lord, into judgment with Thy servants, for in Thy sight shall no man living be justified. But for the sake of Jesus Christ, who His own self bore our sins in His own body on the tree for us, grant us Thy forgiveness, and lift Thou up the light of Thy countenance upon us.

Cause us to have regard to Thy glory in all we think and all we do, and let our chief desire be in all things to please Thee, and to hasten the coming of Thy kingdom.

Teach us to redeem the time, because the days are evil; to give diligence to make our calling and election sure, and to work out our own salvation with fear and trembling.

Teach us to worship Thee spiritually and acceptably, through Christ; to reverence Thy name, and Word, and ordinances; to honour our superiors, and respect our equals and inferiors; to wrong none in their body or estate, but to love and forgive our enemies.

Prepare us for all sufferings, with faith and hope and patience. Strengthen us for the right discharge of every duty. Cause us to overcome in all temptations, and to persevere even unto the end; that having lived soberly, righteously, and godly in this present world, we may be prepared for the next, and may joyfully receive the summons to depart, from having loved and served Thee on earth, to praise and hold fellowship with Thee for ever, through Jesus Christ our Lord and Saviour.

Bestow Thy blessing, we beseech Thee, on our friends and kindred. Keep them from the evil that is in the world. Remember them for good, and visit them with Thy salvation.

Father of mercies, have pity on the afflicted. Relieve their distresses; comfort them in their sorrows; and grant them a happy issue out of all their troubles.

Prepare us, O God, for every trial and for every duty. As our days, so let our strength be. Guide us by Thy counsel while we live, and afterwards receive us into glory, for the Lord Jesus' sake.

OUR Father which art in heaven, Hallowed be Thy name. Thy kingdom come. Thy will be done in earth, as it is in heaven. Give us this day our daily bread. And forgive us our debts, as we forgive our debtors. And lead us not into temptation, but deliver us from evil: For Thine is the kingdom, and the power, and the glory, for ever.—*Amen.*

Thursday Evening.

"Pray without ceasing. In everything give thanks: for this is the will of God in Christ Jesus concerning you."

Let us Pray.

O LORD our God, most high and holy, who humblest Thyself to behold the things that are on earth, and dost not despise the prayer of the penitent, have mercy on us, Thine unworthy children, and hear us when we call on Thee in the name of Jesus Christ our Lord.

We are not worthy to lift up our eyes to heaven, or to take Thy holy name into our lips. Our sins have been many. Our own hearts condemn us on account of them; and Thou art greater than our hearts, and knowest all things.

Lord God, most merciful and gracious, remember not against us, we beseech Thee, the sins of this day. Pardon the vanity of our thoughts, our waywardness of temper, our worldliness of spirit, our want of love to Thee, and of charity to our fellow-men. Justify us freely by Thy grace through the redemption that is in Christ Jesus; and grant us, for His sake, the blessedness of those whose transgression is forgiven, whose sin is covered, and unto whom Thou imputest not iniquity.

Gracious God, who desirest not sacrifice, but requirest of us to do justly, to love mercy, and to walk humbly with Thee, grant us, we pray Thee, the grace of a true repentance; and so direct and govern our hearts and lives, that henceforth we may walk in the way of Thy commandments, and may offer unto Thee sacrifices of righteousness, well-pleasing in Thy sight, through Jesus Christ our Lord.

Teach us to examine and prove ourselves in the

light of Thy Holy Word, that we may not continue in any sin or neglect any duty. Let our rejoicing be the testimony of our conscience, that in simplicity and godly sincerity we have our conversation in the world.

O God, who bearest with our sins and crownest us with Thy loving-kindnesses, give us hearts more sensible of Thy love to us, and more full of love to Thee, and dispose us ever to seek our happiness in the doing of Thy will and in the hope of Thy heavenly kingdom.

Merciful Father, who givest Thy beloved sleep, let our rest this night be quiet and refreshing; and if it please Thee to spare us to see another day, enable us faithfully to spend it in Thy service.

We commend to Thy care our relatives and friends, beseeching Thee to remember them with the favour that Thou bearest unto Thy people, and to visit them with Thy salvation.

[We implore Thy blessing on the children of this family. Preserve them from the sins and dangers of youth. Incline their hearts to seek Thee early; and prepare them for serving Thee here and hereafter.]

Bestow Thy favour on all the members of this household. May we be faithful servants of the Lord Christ, and at last receive of Him the reward of the inheritance.

Father of mercies and God of all comfort, have pity on those whom Thou hast visited with affliction.

Look with compassion on our fellow-men who are sitting in darkness; cause Thy marvellous light to shine upon them; and hasten the time when all the nations of the earth shall be brought to the faith and obedience of Thy Gospel.

Give ear, O God, to our humble supplications, and grant unto us an answer in peace, for the Lord Jesus' sake.

OUR Father which art in heaven, Hallowed be Thy name. Thy kingdom come. Thy will be done in earth, as it is in heaven. Give us this day our daily bread. And forgive us our debts, as we forgive our debtors. And lead us not into temptation, but deliver us from evil: For Thine is the kingdom, and the power, and the glory, for ever.—*Amen.*

Friday Morning.

"O Lord God of heaven, the great and terrible God, that keepeth covenant and mercy for them that love Him and keep His commandments; let Thine ear now be attentive, and Thine eyes open, that Thou mayest hear the prayer of Thy servant, which I pray before Thee now."

LET US PRAY.

O GOD, through whose care we have slept in peace and awaked in safety, we give Thee thanks for all Thy past goodness, and humbly implore Thy continued favour. Thou art our God, early will we seek Thee. Our voice shalt Thou hear in the morning, O Lord; in the morning will we direct our prayer to Thee, and will look up.

We confess before Thee that we are sinful creatures, unworthy to receive any blessing at Thy hands. But we put our trust in Thy well-beloved Son, who gave Himself as a sacrifice for our sins, and ever liveth to make intercession for us; and in His name we beseech Thee to grant us Thy pardon, to aid us with Thy grace, to sanctify our souls for Thy service, and to fulfil every need of ours according to Thy riches in glory in Christ Jesus.

O God, who hast appointed to every man his duty, and art now calling us, in the morning of another day, to go forth to our labour until the evening, teach us in all our ways to acknowledge Thee. Enable us to perform our work with diligence, and to guide our affairs with discretion. And let it please Thee, in all our undertakings, to further us with Thy help, and to grant us such success as seemeth good to Thee.

Teach us, in our dealings with our fellow-men, to walk in truth and uprightness before Thee; rendering unto all their dues, and doing unto others as we would that they should do to us. Dispose us, as much as lieth in us, to live peaceably with all men, to be kindly affectioned one to another, and to do good to all as we have opportunity.

Help us by Thy grace to keep ourselves unspotted from the world. Suffer us not to be overburdened with its cares, ensnared by its pleasures, corrupted by its riches, or led astray by its follies.

Teach us to live above it, and to look beyond it, as pilgrims and strangers on the earth, as all our fathers were.

Keep us chaste in all our thoughts and temperate in all our enjoyments. Suffer us not to be tempted above what we are able to bear, but in every temptation make a way to escape, that we may be able to bear it.

Father of mercies, extend Thy compassion to those who are disabled by sickness and infirmity for engaging in the active business of life. Help them to glorify Thee in their affliction by meek submission to Thy will, and by a firm trust in Thy gracious promise that all things work together for good to them that love Thee.

Bestow Thy favour on our friends and kindred. Deliver them from the evil that is in the world, and keep them by Thy power through faith unto salvation.

Bless all ranks and conditions of men among us. Help them in their several stations faithfully to walk with Thee.

[O God, who blessest the springing of the earth, and crownest the year with Thy goodness, vouchsafe unto us favourable weather and fruitful seasons, that our pastures may be clothed with flocks, and our valleys covered with corn, and our souls may rejoice and be glad in Thee.]

Extend Thy mercy to all our brethren of mankind. Our heart's desire and prayer is, that they may be saved. Let the people praise Thee, O God; let all the people praise Thee.

Grant these requests, O Father, we beseech Thee, and all other things which Thou knowest to be needful for us, according to Thy promises made to us in Jesus Christ, through whom we humbly offer our prayers, and to whom, with Thee and with the Holy Spirit, be glory everlasting.

OUR Father which art in heaven, Hallowed be Thy name. Thy kingdom come. Thy will be done in earth, as it is in heaven. Give us this day our daily bread. And forgive us our debts, as we forgive our debtors. And lead us not into temptation, but deliver us from evil: For Thine is the kingdom, and the power, and the glory, for ever.—*Amen.*

Friday Evening.

"Blessed is the man that walketh not in the counsel of the ungodly, nor standeth in the way of sinners, nor sitteth in the seat of the scornful: but his delight is in the law of the Lord; and in His law doth he meditate day and night."

LET US PRAY.

O LORD, who art good, and ready to forgive, and plenteous in mercy unto all them that call upon Thee, incline Thine ear, we beseech Thee, to our supplications, which we offer in the name of Thy wellbeloved Son. Let our prayer be set forth before Thee as incense, and the lifting up of our hands as the evening sacrifice.

We thank Thee for the help Thou hast given us throughout this day, and we humbly beseech Thee to grant us, during the coming night, such quiet rest as shall enable us on the morrow to go forth again with renewed strength to our appointed labours.

Pardon, O God, our offences against Thee in thought, word, and deed.

Quicken our souls that they cleave not to the dust. Convince us of the vanity of this world.

Lead us to choose Thee as the only satisfying portion, and help us so to pass through the things that are temporal that we may not lose those things which are eternal.

Blessed be Thou, O God and Father of our Lord Jesus Christ, who, according to Thine abundant mercy, hast begotten us again to a lively hope by the resurrection of Jesus Christ from the dead; to an inheritance incorruptible and undefiled, and that fadeth not away, reserved for us in heaven. Grant, we beseech Thee, that, having this hope in us, we may remain steadfast in faith, and may abound in every good work. Having our conversation in heaven, and our life hid with Christ in God, may we rest in the full assurance that when He who is our life shall appear, we also shall appear with Him in glory.

Graciously hear us, O God, while we plead with Thee, not for ourselves only, but also for our brethren. Cause Thy light to shine on those who are in darkness. Bring into the way of truth all who are deceived. Succour the tempted. Raise up the fallen. Provide for the destitute. Comfort the afflicted. Support the dying, and prepare them for their change.

And now, O God, we humbly commit ourselves, and those dear to us, to Thy care. May Thy Spirit be with our spirits during the silent watches of the night. Be merciful to us all, we beseech Thee, and bless us, and make Thy face to shine upon us, for the Lord Jesus' sake.

OUR Father which art in heaven, Hallowed be Thy name. Thy kingdom come. Thy will be done in earth, as it is in heaven. Give us this day our daily bread. And forgive us our debts, as we forgive our debtors. And lead us not into temptation, but deliver us from evil: For Thine is the kingdom, and the power, and the glory, for ever.—*Amen.*

Saturday Morning.

"If my people, which are called by my name, shall humble themselves, and seek my face, and turn from their wicked ways; then will I hear from heaven, and will forgive their sin, and will heal their land."

LET US PRAY.

ALMIGHTY GOD, who inhabitest eternity, but dwellest also with the broken and contrite spirit, incline Thine ear to the voice of our supplications, and pour out upon us the grace of Thy Holy Spirit, that, humbled for our sins, and trembling at Thy Word, we may be revived and comforted with Thy fellowship, and may render unto Thee acceptable worship; through Jesus Christ our Lord.

Remember not, we beseech Thee, our manifold offences, by reason of which we are unworthy to lift up our eyes to the place where Thine honour dwelleth. Graciously forgive us, for the sake of Thy beloved Son, and through Him let it please Thee to bestow upon us the grace of Thy Holy Spirit, whereby we may be disposed and enabled truly to love Thee, heartily to trust in Thee, and wholly to give ourselves to Thy service.

O Lord, who hast called us to be holy because Thou art holy, fulfil in us, we beseech Thee, all the good pleasure of Thy goodness, and stablish us in every good work. Create in us a clean heart, O God, and renew a right spirit within us. Deliver us from evil thoughts, unholy passions, and uncharitable tempers; from pride and vanity, from malice and revenge, from envy and discontent, from covetousness and worldliness. Cause us to abound more and more in faith, and love, and temperance, and godliness. Strengthen in us all holy desires, all good purposes, all kind and brotherly affections, that the name of our Lord Jesus Christ may be glorified in us and we in Him. O God of peace, sanctify us wholly. And grant that our whole spirit and soul and body may be established in holiness before Thee, and preserved blameless unto the coming of our Lord Jesus Christ with all His saints.

Graciously hear us, O God, while we plead with Thee for all whom we ought to remember in our prayers. We commend our friends to Thy favour, our benefactors to Thy bounty, our enemies to Thy forgiveness.

[We pray for the children of this family. May they be lambs of the flock of Christ, tended, fed, and saved by the Good Shepherd.]

We pray for all the members of this household. May we all be able to discharge our different duties in Thy fear with all fidelity.

We beseech Thee to look with compassion on the afflicted, and to grant them all needful consolation and relief. We pray for the dying, that it may please Thee to comfort and sustain them when flesh and heart are failing. We pray for all men, that Thou wouldst enlighten and convert them, until the whole world be filled with Thy glory.

And now, O God, we commit ourselves to Thee. Aid us this day in our several occupations. And whatsoever we do, in word or deed, enable us to do all in the name of the Lord Jesus, through whom we humbly offer our prayers, and to whom, with Thee and with the Holy Spirit, be all honour and glory, for evermore.

OUR Father which art in heaven, Hallowed be Thy name. Thy kingdom come. Thy will be done in earth, as it is in heaven. Give us this day our daily bread. And forgive us our debts, as we forgive our debtors. And lead us not into temptation, but deliver us from evil: For Thine is the kingdom, and the power, and the glory, for ever.—*Amen.*

Saturday Evening.

"I will extol Thee, my God, O King; and I will bless Thy name for ever and ever. Every day will I bless Thee; and I will praise Thy name for ever and ever."

Let us Pray.

HEAVENLY FATHER, who hast brought us to the close of another day and of another week, help us to look back with gratitude on all the way by which Thou hast led us, and on all the care and kindness Thou hast shown us. Make us truly thankful, we beseech Thee, for the preservation of our lives and the supply of our daily wants; for health of body and soundness of mind; for the blessing of home and kindred; for strength and skill to labour, and for whatever success may have crowned our labours; above all, for Thy patience in bearing with our manifold sins, and Thy mercy in continuing to us the means of grace and the hope of glory.

O Lord our God, who desirest not the death of a sinner, but rather that he should turn to Thee and live, grant that Thy goodness may lead us to repentance.

Humble us while we think of all the evil we have done, and of all the good we have omitted to do.

Teach us to reflect, with godly sorrow, on the time we have wasted, the talents we have abused, the privileges and opportunities we have neglected.

Help us, under a deep conviction of our sinfulness, to put our trust in Thy well-beloved Son, in whom alone we have redemption through His blood.

For His sake pardon our manifold offences and give us Thy Holy Spirit, that, being restored to the enjoyment of Thy favour, and renewed in holiness after Thine image, we may live to the praise and glory of Thy name.

O God, who hast made our days as an handbreadth, so that our age is as nothing before Thee, impress us with a sense of our frailty. So teach us to number our days that we may apply our hearts unto wisdom; and while week after week swiftly passes, dispose us to redeem the time, and to give heed to the things which belong unto our peace, lest they be hid for ever from our eyes. Enable us to imitate Christ, our great Example. Teach us to be sober, watchful, and prayerful; and grant that after having done and suffered Thy will upon the earth, we may depart in peace, and may have an entrance ministered to us abundantly into the everlasting kingdom of our Lord and Saviour Jesus Christ.

Hear our prayers, we beseech Thee, for those whom we ought to remember at a throne of grace. Bless all who are in offices of trust and of authority, and aid them with Thy grace.

Look down in pity on the sick and the afflicted; comfort and relieve them according to their necessities. Gather and number them with the blessed, and over-rule Thy chastening for their eternal good.

Have mercy on all the family of mankind. Diffuse among them the knowledge of Thy Gospel, and cause them to receive it in faith and love.

We commend ourselves and all who are dear to us to Thy care this night. Give us the sleep of Thy beloved, and protect us by Thy power; and, if it please Thee, spare us to see the light of Thy holy day, and fit us for the profitable discharge of its solemn duties.

These our humble supplications we present before Thee, O Thou that hearest prayer. Graciously answer them, for the sake of Jesus Christ, to whom, with

Thee and with the Holy Spirit, be honour and glory, for evermore.

OUR Father which art in heaven, Hallowed be Thy name. Thy kingdom come. Thy will be done in earth, as it is in heaven. Give us this day our daily bread. And forgive us our debts, as we forgive our debtors. And lead us not into temptation, but deliver us from evil: For Thine is the kingdom, and the power, and the glory, for ever.—*Amen.*

SECOND WEEK.

Lord's Day Morning.

"O taste and see that the Lord is good: blessed is the man that trusteth in Him."

"O love the Lord, all ye His saints: for the Lord preserveth the faithful."

LET US PRAY.

O LORD our God, who hast commanded us to remember the Sabbath-day and keep it holy, enable us to sanctify this day by resting from the cares and pleasures of the world, and by giving ourselves up to Thy service. Teach us to call the Sabbath a delight, and grant us in the observance of it a foretaste of those heavenly joys which Thou wilt hereafter bestow upon Thy people, through Christ our Lord.

Thou art worthy, O God, to receive blessing, and honour, and thanksgiving. Thy power hath created us; Thy bounty hath sustained us; Thy patience hath spared us; Thy love hath redeemed us. Blessed be Thou, who daily loadest us with benefits, O God of our salvation.

O God, who knowest all our frailty and folly, and from whom our sins are not hid, have mercy upon us after Thy loving-kindness, and according to the multitude of Thy tender mercies, blot out our transgressions. Forgive us all the evil we have done; condemn us not for the good we have omitted to do; but, for the sake of Thy beloved Son, in whom we have redemption, receive us graciously, and love us freely.

Almighty God, who workest in us to will and to do of Thy good pleasure, give us grace, that we may truly repent of our sins, and heartily yield ourselves to Thy service. Let it be the work of our lives to obey Thee—the joy of our souls to please Thee—the satisfaction of our desires, and the fulfilment of our hopes, to walk with Thee in the comforts of Thy fellowship, and to dwell with Thee in the glories of Thy kingdom.

O God, who art light, and in whom is no darkness at all, shine into our hearts, we beseech Thee, by Thy Holy Spirit, and cause us, in Thy light, clearly to see light. Deliver us from ignorance, error, and unbelief; dispose us, as children of the light and of the day, to renounce the hidden things of shame, and by the purity of our lives to commend ourselves to every man's conscience in Thy sight. May our fellowship be with Thee the Father, and with Thy Son Jesus Christ; and when the shadows of this life have passed away, grant that we may enjoy the vision of Thy heavenly glory, and may ourselves shine forth with the brightness of the sun, in Thy kingdom for ever and ever. Teach us evermore to look to Christ, that unto us He may appear the second time without sin unto salvation.

Almighty God, who hast spared us in Thy providence to see another return of Thy holy day, make us thankful for this season of hallowed rest; and enable us by Thy grace to sanctify it, to the honour of Thy name and the good of our souls. Cause us to rejoice when it is said unto us, Go ye up into the house of the Lord; and teach us to esteem a day spent in Thy courts as better than a thousand. Give grace to Thy ministering servants, that they may handle aright the Word of truth; and let their preaching be in the demonstration of the Spirit and of power.

Draw nigh to those who are necessarily withheld from worshipping Thee in the congregation of Thy people, and make them glad with the light of Thy countenance. Have pity on those who neglect Thine ordinances; cause them yet to seek Thee whilst Thou art to be found, and to call upon Thee whilst Thou art near. Look with compassion on the whole family of man. Send forth the light of the Gospel into every land, and pour out Thy Spirit upon all flesh, that Thy righteousness may be openly shown in the sight of the heathen, and that the whole earth may be filled with Thy glory.

These, our humble supplications, we present to Thee, in the name of Jesus, Thy beloved Son, to whom, with Thee and with the Holy Spirit, be honour and praise, dominion and blessing, for ever and ever.

OUR Father which art in heaven, Hallowed be Thy name. Thy kingdom come. Thy will be done in earth, as it is in heaven. Give us this day our daily bread. And forgive us our debts, as we forgive our debtors. And lead us not into temptation, but deliver us from evil: For Thine is the kingdom, and the power, and the glory, for ever.—*Amen.*

Lord's Day Evening.

"It is a good thing to give thanks unto the Lord, and to sing praises unto Thy name, O Most High: to show forth Thy loving-kindness in the morning, and Thy faithfulness every night."

LET US PRAY.

ALMIGHTY GOD, who hast permitted us to enjoy the holy rest of the Lord's Day, and the blessedness of the man whom Thou causest to approach unto Thee, that he may dwell in Thy courts, we give Thee thanks for the privileges Thou hast given, and humbly pray that we may profit by the use of them.

We bless Thee that we have a great High Priest who can be touched with the feeling of our infirmities, and we beseech Thee to pardon for His sake the manifold sins of our sacred duties. Graciously receive the tribute of our worship; and grant that the saving truths of Thy Word may be fixed in our memories and impressed upon our hearts, that, as precious seed sown in a good soil, they may bring forth fruit abundantly to Thy praise.

O our God, we have cause to be ashamed that

hitherto we have profited so little by the lessons of Thy Word and the worship of Thy house. Let them not rise against us to our condemnation; but grant that we may grow in knowledge and in grace, according to the opportunities and advantages Thou hast afforded us, and that by our continual advancement in godliness we may be enabled to show forth the praises of Him who hath called us out of darkness into His marvellous light.

Almighty God and Saviour, in whom all fulness dwells, we humbly beseech Thee that we may receive of Thy fulness grace sufficient for us; so that, being taught of Thee, we may abound more and more in all goodness. Fill us with the knowledge of Thy will. Perfect our repentance. Strengthen our faith. Enliven our hope. Increase our love. Suffer us not to rest satisfied with present attainments; but carry us forward in the path of duty, until we are fit to be translated to that better country where, being fully conformed to Thine image, we shall see Thee face to face.

And, seeing we know not the day nor the hour when the Lord shall appear, give us grace that we may be ready to meet Him when He comes in His glory.

We pray for all our brethren of mankind, that they may be brought to a knowledge of the truth. Be merciful to the land in which we dwell. Bless our Sovereign and her family. Be gracious to all who minister in holy things.

Visit in mercy the children of affliction; supply their wants; relieve their sufferings; give unto them patience; and in Thy good time deliver them from all their troubles.

Take us, we beseech Thee, and all who are dear to us, under Thy fatherly protection this night. Defend us from danger; grant us quiet sleep; and, if it please Thee, spare us to enjoy the blessings and to discharge the duties of another day.

Graciously hear us, O God, and have mercy on us, for the sake of Thy beloved Son, our Strength and our Redeemer.

OUR Father which art in heaven, Hallowed be Thy name. Thy kingdom come. Thy will be done in earth, as it is in heaven. Give us this day our daily bread. And forgive us our debts, as we forgive our debtors. And lead us not into temptation, but deliver us from evil: For Thine is the kingdom, and the power, and the glory, for ever.—*Amen.*

Monday Morning.

"Let my cry come near before Thee, O Lord: give me understanding according to Thy word.

"Let my supplication come before Thee: deliver me according to Thy word.

"My lips shall utter praise, when Thou hast taught me Thy statutes."

Let us Pray.

ALMIGHTY GOD, our heavenly Father, who hast safely brought us to the beginning of this day, continue to us throughout the course of it Thy fatherly guidance and protection. Defend us from all danger; keep us from all sin; and so direct and govern us by Thy Holy Spirit, that we may walk in uprightness before Thee, and do always that which is pleasing in Thy sight.

We confess, O God, that we are prone to forget Thee amidst the business of our daily life, and that we have in many things offended Thee by our disobedience. Pardon, we beseech Thee, for the sake of Thy beloved Son, our manifold sins and shortcomings in the time that is past; and enable us henceforth more constantly to remember Thee, and with greater diligence and faithfulness to serve Thee.

Help us to enter on the labours of the week in the spirit of that worship which we yesterday rendered unto Thee in Thy house, and of those holy lessons which were addressed to us from Thy Word. Teach us to acknowledge Thee in all our ways. Whether we be called to command or to obey, to teach or to learn, to labour or to endure, enable us in our several callings to abide with Thee. And whatsoever we do, dispose us to do it heartily, as unto Thee and not unto men.

Father of mercies, receive our thanks for all the benefits, temporal and spiritual, which from day to day Thou art graciously bestowing on us; and enable us to show our gratitude, not only by the praises of our lips, but by the cheerful obedience of our hearts and lives.

Prepare us, O Christ, for Thy coming. When Thou comest quickly, may we be found watching, ready to say,—Even so come, Lord Jesus.

[To Thy fatherly care, O God, we commend the children of this family. Preserve them from the dangers and temptations to which, in an evil world, they are exposed. Cause them to grow in grace, and in the knowledge of Jesus Christ, whom to know is life eternal.]

Give the protection of Thy presence to all who dwell in this house, that Thou mayest be known to be the Defender of this family and the Inhabitant of this dwelling. Grant unto us all as Thy servants, health of body and soul, that we may love Thee with all our strength, and with perfect affection fulfil Thy pleasure through Jesus Christ our Lord.

Graciously hear our intercessions, O God, for the Queen and all in authority, that they may rule as Thy servants; and for the ministers in the Church, that they may be faithful and successful.

We pray for our friends and kindred, that it may please Thee to remember them for good and to visit them with Thy salvation; for those who are in adversity and affliction, that they may be blessed with the comforts of Thy Word and Spirit; and for all men, that they may be brought to the knowledge, faith, and obedience of Thy Gospel.

These our humble supplications we present to Thee, O Thou that hearest prayer. Graciously answer them for the sake of Jesus Christ, our Lord and Saviour.

OUR Father which art in heaven, Hallowed be Thy name. Thy kingdom come. Thy will be done in earth, as it is in heaven. Give us this day our daily bread. And forgive us our debts, as we forgive our debtors. And lead us not into temptation, but deliver us from evil: For Thine is the kingdom, and the power, and the glory, for ever.—*Amen.*

Monday Evening.

"The Lord shall preserve Thee from all evil: He shall preserve thy soul.

"The Lord shall preserve thy going out, and thy coming in, from this time forth, and even for evermore."

Let us Pray.

ALMIGHTY GOD, who art the confidence of all the ends of the earth, and of them that are afar off upon the sea—our sun and shield, our refuge and defence, the strength of our heart and the rock of our salvation—enable us to put our trust in Thee. Teach us with full assurance to look up to Thee as our reconciled God and Father in Christ Jesus, and graciously remember Thy word unto Thy servants, on which Thou hast caused us to hope, that Thou wilt keep him in perfect peace whose mind is stayed on Thee.

Pardon, O God, whatever want of confidence we have shown towards Thee, and lead us henceforth by the teaching of Thy Holy Spirit to trust in Thee with all our heart. Help us to rely on the goodness of Thy providence. Increase our faith in the promises of Thy Word. Dispose us to cast upon Thee all our cares, humbly to commit to Thy keeping all our interests, and earnestly to seek the guidance of Thy wisdom and the aid of Thy strength in all our undertakings.

Teach us, O God of all grace, wholly to depend on

the merciful provisions of Thy Gospel. Counting all things but loss for the excellency of the knowledge of Christ Jesus our Lord, may we seek to win Christ, and to be found in Him, having the righteousness which is by faith. Convince us that without Him we can do nothing, but that through His strength we can do all things. May we be persuaded that neither death, nor life, nor angels, nor principalities, nor powers, nor things present, nor things to come, nor height, nor depth, nor any other creature, shall be able to separate us from the love of God, which is in Christ Jesus our Lord.

Hear our prayers for our kindred and our friends. Deliver them from evil, preserve them in all good, and bring them to everlasting joy.

Bless our neighbours, and all with whom we are associated in the work of life. Sustain them by Thy grace, and enable us all to help one another on the way to heaven.

Succour those who are in distress. Reveal Thy marvellous light to such as are in darkness. Increase everywhere the number of Thy faithful people; and let all those that trust in Thee rejoice, because with favour Thou dost compass them as with a shield.

And now, O God, we commend ourselves to Thy care. We will lay ourselves down in peace and sleep, because Thou only makest us to dwell in safety.

Graciously hear the voice of our supplications, which we offer in the name of Thy well-beloved Son, our Lord and Saviour.

OUR Father which art in heaven, Hallowed be Thy name. Thy kingdom come. Thy will be done in earth, as it is in heaven. Give us this day our daily bread. And forgive us our debts, as we forgive our debtors. And lead us not into temptation, but deliver us from evil: For Thine is the kingdom, and the power, and the glory, for ever.—*Amen.*

Tuesday Morning.

"Labour not for the meat which perisheth, but for that meat which endureth unto everlasting life, which the Son of man shall give unto you."

LET US PRAY.

O GOD, who hast taught us to be careful for nothing, but in everything, by prayer and supplication with thanksgiving, to make our requests known unto Thee, we cast ourselves this morning on Thy care, and humbly ask of Thee those things which are necessary as well for the body as the soul.

Holy Father, by reason of our manifold offences we are not worthy to come into Thy presence. But we put our trust in the merits of Thy beloved Son, who gave Himself a sacrifice for our sins; and for His sake we earnestly beseech Thee to take away all our iniquity, to receive us graciously, and to supply all our need.

O God, who knowest our wants, and hast graciously promised to them that seek first Thy kingdom and the righteousness thereof, that all other things shall be added to them, grant us such earthly blessings as Thy wisdom seeth to be expedient for us. Give us neither poverty nor riches; feed us with food convenient for us,—lest we be full and deny Thee, and say, Who is the Lord? or lest we be poor, and steal, and take the name of the Lord in vain.

Make us to be heartily content with Thy blessed will.

Suffer us not in prosperity to forget Thee, or in adversity to think ourselves forgotten of Thee. May the trial of our faith be found unto praise, and honour, and glory, at the appearing of Jesus Christ our Lord. Teach us to thank Thee for all Thy gifts; and when earthly comforts fail, to rejoice the more in the God of our salvation.

Above all, grant that our spiritual wants may be abundantly supplied out of the fulness of the Gospel, to the end that our souls, growing in knowledge and in grace, may be strengthened and nourished unto life eternal.

We pray not only for ourselves, but for our brethren, that it may please Thee to succour them according to their several necessities. Give food to the hungry, clothing to the naked, instruction to the ignorant, comfort to the sorrowful, health to the sick, and hope to the dying.

Hear our prayers for the prayerless, and save the impenitent, that they perish not eternally. Deliver the heathen from their idolatry, the Jews from their unbelief, and the followers of the false prophet from their misbelief. Accomplish the number of thine elect, O God, and brighten Thy world speedily with the glory of Christ.

Bestow Thy blessing on the labours of the artisan and the husbandman; bless our trade and commerce. [Grant unto us favourable weather and fruitful seasons, that our fields may in due time yield an abundant increase.]

Bless our native land with plenty and prosperity. Enrich with Thy favour our Sovereign the Queen. Give to all ranks and conditions of the people such temporal and spiritual blessings as are needful for them.

Hear us, O God, and grant an answer of peace, for the sake of Thy beloved Son, our Lord and Saviour.

OUR Father which art in heaven, Hallowed be Thy name. Thy kingdom come. Thy will be done in earth, as it is in heaven. Give us this day our daily bread. And forgive us our debts, as we forgive our debtors. And lead us not into temptation, but deliver us from evil: For Thine is the kingdom, and the power, and the glory, for ever.—*Amen.*

Tuesday Evening.

"I will say of the Lord, He is my refuge and my fortress: my God; in Him will I trust. Thou shalt not be afraid for the terror by night; nor for the arrow that flieth by day. Because thou hast made the Lord which is my refuge, even the Most High, thy habitation; there shall no evil befall thee, neither shall any plague come nigh thy dwelling."

Let us Pray.

ALMIGHTY GOD, who orderest all things in heaven and on earth according to Thy wise counsel, give us grace that we may reverently adore Thee and cheerfully submit to Thy most blessed will. Teach us to acknowledge that Thou art just in all Thy ways and holy in all Thy works; and although clouds and darkness are about Thee, enable us to rejoice that righteousness and judgment are the habitation of Thy throne, and that mercy and truth go before Thy face.

We confess, O God, that we have been slow to own the wisdom and goodness of Thy dealings with us; that we have often been discontented with our own condition, and have looked with envy and uncharitableness on the good of others; and that, instead of meekly bowing to Thy will, we have often, by our discontent, rebelled against Thee.

Pardon, O God, wherein we have thus offended Thee. Graciously receive us through the merits of Thy beloved Son, in whom we have redemption and salvation. Forgive, for His sake, our many provocations, and remember our iniquities no more.

Give us grace also, whereby we may be enabled wholly to give ourselves up to Thy disposal. Make us willing that Thou shouldst choose our portion for us. Confirm our faith in the assurance Thou hast given us that all Thy ways are mercy and truth to such as keep Thy covenant and Thy testimonies, and that all things work together for good to them that love Thee. Teach us, in whatsoever state we are, therewith to be content, that everywhere and in all things we may be instructed both to be full and to be hungry, both to abound and to suffer need.

O God, who hast prepared for us in heaven a better and more enduring inheritance than can be found on earth, dispose us to seek those things which are above; and enable us so to look at the things which are unseen and eternal, that we may bear patiently all present hardships, and may reckon them unworthy to be compared with the glory which shall hereafter be revealed in us.

Father of mercies, we thankfully acknowledge Thy goodness to us throughout this day; and we humbly commit ourselves, and all whom we love, to Thy fatherly protection during this night. Suffer no evil to befall us, nor any plague to come nigh our dwelling.

We pray for the members of this household, that we may prosper in all things and be in health; above all, that our souls may prosper.

We pray for the sick, the sorrowful, and the dying, that it may please Thee to comfort and support them.

We pray for the whole family of mankind, that Thou wouldst mercifully enlighten and convert them, and bless them in Christ Jesus with spiritual and heavenly blessings.

Incline Thine ear, O God, to our supplications, which we offer in the name of Thy beloved Son, our Lord and only Saviour.

OUR Father which art in heaven, Hallowed be Thy name. Thy kingdom come. Thy will be done in earth, as it is in heaven. Give us this day our

daily bread. And forgive us our debts, as we forgive our debtors. And lead us not into temptation, but deliver us from evil: For Thine is the kingdom, and the power, and the glory, for ever.—*Amen.*

Wednesday Morning.

"Cause me to hear Thy loving-kindness in the morning; for in Thee do I trust: cause me to know the way wherein I should walk; for I lift up my soul unto Thee."

LET US PRAY.

O GOD, who by the entrance of Thy words givest light to the simple, fill us, we beseech Thee, with the knowledge of Thy will in all wisdom and spiritual understanding, that we may walk worthy of Thee unto all pleasing, and may be fruitful in every good work, through Jesus Christ our Lord.

We beseech Thee, O Lord, in Thy compassion to give us true faith in Thee, through Jesus Christ our Lord. May we trust Thee with all our heart, and ever render unto Thee a faithful service. Enable us to believe those truths which are essential to our salvation, and which alone can establish in us virtue.

O Thou that hearest prayer, unto Thee shall all flesh come. We thank Thee that we have a great High Priest, who ever liveth to make intercession for us, and in His name we earnestly beseech Thee to pardon our sins, to help our infirmities, and to bestow upon us whatsoever things Thou knowest to be needful or expedient for us.

Lord, we believe; help Thou our unbelief. Pardon the weakness and unsteadfastness of our faith. Make it more firm and lively and effectual, that we may be filled with all joy and peace in believing, and may be fruitful in every good work.

God of all grace, enable us this day, and all the days of our sojourning in the body, to live by faith in the Son of God, who loved us, and gave Himself for us. Give us grace continually to abide in Him, that we may bear much fruit. Whatsoever we do, in word or deed, dispose us to do all in the name of the Lord Jesus, giving thanks to our God, even Thee our Father, by Him.

May we be holy in conversation, and godly, looking for and hastening unto the coming of the day of God.

Guide and strengthen us by Thy Holy Spirit, that we may be faithful to all our responsibilities, honest in all our dealings, and gentle in our communications with all men. May we be able to preserve an even temper and the spirit of Christian charity amid all the anxieties of our business and the trials of our daily life.

Graciously hear our intercessions, we beseech Thee, for those whom we ought to remember at Thy throne of grace. Bestow Thy favour on our friends. Give relief and comfort to the afflicted. Instruct the ignorant; reclaim the erring; build up Thy saints in their most holy faith.

[Bestow Thy blessing on the children of this family. Keep them from the snares and dangers of an evil world; and cause them to grow in knowledge and in grace.]

Bless our Queen, and all in authority over us. Extend Thy favour and protection to our country. Bless Thy whole Church throughout the world. Watch over Thy flock wherever scattered, and in Thine infinite mercy be pleased to gather all at last into the one heavenly fold.

These our humble supplications we present to Thee, in the name and through the mediation of Jesus Christ, our Lord and Saviour.

OUR Father which art in heaven, Hallowed be Thy name. Thy kingdom come. Thy will be done in earth, as it is in heaven. Give us this day our daily bread. And forgive us our debts, as we forgive our debtors. And lead us not into temptation, but deliver us from evil: For Thine is the kingdom, and the power, and the glory, for ever.—*Amen.*

Wednesday Evening.

"O Lord God of my salvation, I have cried day and night before Thee. Let my prayer come before Thee: incline Thine ear unto my cry."

LET US PRAY.

O GOD, who hast taught us to be careful for nothing, but in everything, by prayer and supplication with thanksgiving, to make our requests known unto Thee, pour out upon us the spirit of grace and supplication, and enable us so to cast our care upon Thee, that Thy peace, which passeth understanding, may keep our hearts and minds through Christ Jesus, to whom, with Thee and the Holy Spirit, be glory everlasting.

Teach us, O God, to love Thee with all our heart, and with all our soul, and with all our mind, that, living ever in holy sympathy with Thee, we may be constrained to love what Thou dost love, and to do good to all men as we have opportunity.

We acknowledge, O God, that our hearts have been estranged from Thee; that we have been regardless of Thy goodness, indifferent to Thine excellences, and unthankful for Thy benefits; that we have allowed the sins and vanities of the world to rob Thee of our affection, and that we have preferred the indulgence of our sinful desires to the enjoyment of Thy favour and loving-kindness.

Merciful Father, who hast given Thine own Son to be the propitiation for our sins, grant us, for His sake, Thy mercy to forgive us and Thy grace to help us. Pardon all the defects of our love to Thee, and all the excess of our love for earthly things. Turn our inclinations and affections from those vain objects which would draw away our hearts from Thee. Give to us clear views of Thine excellency, and impress us with a lively sense of Thy goodness. Above all, teach us to comprehend, with all saints, the breadth, and length, and depth, and height of Thy love towards us in Jesus Christ.

God of all grace, without whom we can do nothing, enable us to continue in Thy love; and cause our love to abound yet more and more, that we may prefer Thy favour above our chief joy. May we delight to do Thy blessed will, and may we be filled with the fruits of righteousness, which are by Jesus Christ unto Thy praise and glory.

Father of mercies, we give Thee special thanks for the love Thou hast this day conferred upon us. And we beseech Thee this night to keep us and all who are dear to us safe under Thy protection.

O God, who art very pitiful and of tender mercy, look with compassion on all who are afflicted. Heal the sick; provide for the destitute; deliver the oppressed; prepare the dying for their change.

Let Thy way, O God, be known upon the earth, and Thy saving health among all nations. Gather the dispersed of Israel, with the fulness of the Gentiles, into Thy fold, and add to Thy Church daily such as shall be saved.

Mercifully hear us, O God, and accept of us, for the Lord Jesus' sake.

OUR Father which art in heaven, Hallowed be Thy name. Thy kingdom come. Thy will be done in earth, as it is in heaven. Give us this day our daily bread. And forgive us our debts, as we forgive our debtors. And lead us not into temptation, but deliver us from evil: For Thine is the kingdom, and the power, and the glory, for ever.—*Amen.*

Thursday Morning.

"Wait on the Lord; be of good courage, and He shall strengthen thine heart: wait, I say, on the Lord."

Let us Pray.

O GOD, who hast taught us to approach Thee as children to a Father able and ready to help us, send forth, we humbly beseech Thee, the Spirit of Thy Son into our hearts, that we may now draw near unto Thee with all holy reverence and confidence, and may by faith obtain the petitions which we ask of Thee, through Jesus Christ our Lord.

O our God, we are ashamed to lift up our faces unto Thee; for our consciences accuse us and our sins witness against us. We confess that our hearts are corrupt, and that there is no soundness in us. We acknowledge that there is a law in our members, warring against the law of our mind, and bringing us into captivity to the law of sin. We lament that when we would do good evil is present with us; and that through the power of the sins that beset us, we are often turned from Thy ways, and led to do that which is hateful in Thy sight.

Father of mercies, we beseech Thee to have compassion on us. Be pleased, for the sake of Jesus Christ, Thy well-beloved Son, to blot out all our sins; and to bestow upon us the grace of Thy Holy Spirit, whereby we may be renewed after Thine image, and may die unto sin and live unto righteousness. Enable us to crucify the flesh, with its evil desires and affections; and grant that, being made free from sin, and having become servants to God, we may have our fruit unto holiness, and the end everlasting life.

Almighty God, who givest power to the faint and increasest strength to them that have no might, we look to Thee for aid in all our duties and in all our trials. Fulfil to us, now and always, Thy promise, that as our days so shall our strength be. Arm us with might to resist every temptation, and stablish our hearts in every good word and work, that we may stand perfect and complete in Thy will.

Guide us in all that we think and say and do this day, that all may be to Thy glory. Keep us amid all the temptations which may beset us at home and abroad, and grant that we may so behave ourselves, that men may know that we are Thy servants, and ruled by Thy holy will.

Bestow Thy favour, we beseech Thee, on our friends and kindred. Bless them and keep them, and make Thy face to shine upon them. Extend Thy pity to the sick and the afflicted. Comfort the mourners. Prepare the dying for death, and give them assurance of their safety in Jesus Christ.

O God, who wouldst have all men to come to the knowledge of the truth, let Thy Word everywhere have free course and be glorified; and hasten the time when all the kingdoms of this world shall become the kingdoms of our Lord and of His Christ.

Graciously hear us, O God, and accept of us, through Jesus Christ, our only Mediator, to whom, with Thee and with the Holy Spirit, be glory everlasting.

OUR Father which art in heaven, Hallowed be Thy name. Thy kingdom come. Thy will be done in earth, as it is in heaven. Give us this day our daily bread. And forgive us our debts, as we forgive our debtors. And lead us not into temptation, but deliver us from evil: For Thine is the kingdom, and the power, and the glory, for ever.—*Amen.*

Thursday Evening.

"For as many as are led by the Spirit of God, they are the sons of God."

"The Spirit itself beareth witness with our spirit, that we are the children of God."

LET US PRAY.

O THOU that dwellest in the heavens, unto Thee do we lift up our souls. We thank Thee for the encouragement Thou hast given us to come with boldness unto the throne of grace; and for the assurance that if we, being evil, know how to give good gifts unto our children, much more wilt Thou, our heavenly Father, give Thy Holy Spirit to them that ask Thee.

Grant us, we pray Thee, this great gift. Let Thy Spirit be shed on us abundantly through Jesus Christ our Saviour. Let Him be unto us a Spirit of light and truth, to guide us to the understanding of Thy mind and will; a Spirit of power, to quicken us, and to strengthen us with all might in the inner man; a Spirit of comfort, to cheer us in our times of trouble; and a Spirit of holiness, to purify us more and more, and to make us fruitful in every good work.

Pardon, O God, wherein we have offended Thee by

grieving or resisting Thy Spirit. Suffer us not to do despite unto Him, lest He should cease to strive with us any more. Cast us not away from Thy presence, and take not Thy Holy Spirit from us, but grant that He may abide with us continually, making us to grow in knowledge and in grace.

O God our Father, who hast called us unto the adoption of children by Jesus Christ, and hast given us in Him exceeding great and precious promises, we earnestly pray that Thy Holy Spirit may witness with our spirits that we are Thy children.

Hear our intercessions, O God, in behalf of all our brethren of mankind. Pour out Thy Holy Spirit upon all flesh, that the wilderness may become a fruitful field, and that the whole earth may be filled with Thy glory. Pour out Thy Holy Spirit upon all the Churches, that Thy work may appear in them. Impart the consolations of Thy Spirit to all whom Thou hast afflicted, that they may be strengthened, according to His glorious power, unto all patience and long-suffering with joyfulness. Give unto all Thy people, we beseech Thee, the grace of Thy Holy Spirit in such measure as Thy divine wisdom seeth to be needful to build them up in their most holy faith, and enable them steadfastly to abide with Thee, looking for that blessed hope and the glorious appearing of the great God and our Saviour Jesus Christ.

We thank Thee for the mercies of the day; for strength to labour and for reason to guide us in our temporal concerns; and above all, for the heavenly light which Thou hast caused to shine upon us, showing us the true way to the heavenly country.

And now, O God, we humbly commit ourselves, and

all whom we love, to Thy fatherly care. Grant us refreshing sleep; shield us from all evil; and bring us in peace to the light of a new day.

Graciously hear us, O God, and have mercy upon us, for the Lord Jesus' sake.

OUR Father which art in heaven, Hallowed be Thy name. Thy kingdom come. Thy will be done in earth, as it is in heaven. Give us this day our daily bread. And forgive us our debts, as we forgive our debtors. And lead us not into temptation, but deliver us from evil: For Thine is the kingdom, and the power, and the glory, for ever.—*Amen.*

Friday Morning.

"I will love Thee, O Lord, my strength. The Lord is my rock, and my fortress, and my deliverer; my God, my strength, in whom I will trust; my buckler, and the horn of my salvation, and my strong tower. I will call upon the Lord, who is worthy to be praised."

LET US PRAY.

ALMIGHTY GOD, who dwellest in the light to which no man can approach; in whose presence there is no night, in the light of whose countenance there is perpetual day; we, Thy servants, whom Thou hast preserved during the past night, and who live by Thy power, desire this morning to bless Thee for the defence of Thy watchful providence ; and humbly pray Thee to grant that this day, and all the days of our life, may be holy and peaceable, healthful to our bodies and profitable to our souls.

O Lord our God, we are sinful creatures, unworthy of Thy favour, but we are sorrowful and repentant. And though Thou hast just cause to be angry with us, yet in Christ Jesus hath Thine anger been turned away. Be pleased, O God, for the sake of Thy beloved Son, to blot out all our sins from Thy remembrance, and to heal our souls that we may sin against Thee no more. Open our eyes that we may see our infirmities ; make us watchful against them ; enable us to overcome them ; and give us perfect understanding in the way of godliness, that we may walk in it all the days of our pilgrimage. Dispose us to be faithful and diligent in our several callings ; cheerful and zealous in duty ; patient in trial ; charitable in temper ; pure and sincere in speech ; fervent in prayer, and ready to every good work. And whether we eat or drink, or whatsoever we do, enable us to do all to Thy glory.

Let Thy good providence continually watch over us, that we may be delivered from all evil. Enable us so to spend this day that it may be profitable both to ourselves and others ; and grant that we may, throughout our whole life, be so directed and governed by Thy Holy Spirit, that when the time of our sojourn on earth is ended, we may die in Thy favour, rest in a holy hope, and finally obtain the joys of a blessed resurrection.

Regard with Thy favour this family and neighbourhood. Prosper our country. Protect our Queen. Guide all in authority. Bless Thy Church Universal.

Unite the hearts of all Thy faithful people in the belief and love of Thy truth, and hasten the prevalence of Thy kingdom among all nations.

God of all comfort, have pity on the afflicted; assuage their griefs; relieve their sufferings; and overrule Thy chastening for their good.

Graciously hear and answer us, O Lord, according to the fulness of Thy mercy in Christ Jesus, our Lord and Saviour.

OUR Father which art in heaven, Hallowed be Thy name. Thy kingdom come. Thy will be done in earth, as it is in heaven. Give us this day our daily bread. And forgive us our debts, as we forgive our debtors. And lead us not into temptation, but deliver us from evil: For Thine is the kingdom, and the power, and the glory, for ever.—*Amen.*

Friday Evening.

"Blessed is he whose transgression is forgiven and whose sin is covered."

LET US PRAY.

ETERNAL GOD, Father of men and angels, by whose care and providence we are preserved and blessed, comforted and assisted, we heartily thank Thee for the many temporal and spiritual mercies

Thou hast bestowed upon us this day. Suffer us not to be forgetful of Thy benefits; and though we are not worthy of the least of them, be pleased still to remember us for good.

Pardon, we beseech Thee, for the sake of Thy beloved Son, the sins we have this day committed against Thee; the unprofitableness of our services, the strength of our evil passions, the uncharitableness of our tempers, the rashness of our words, and the vanity and evil of our actions. Let us never return to those iniquities of which we are ashamed, and which bring sorrow and death. Give us command over our evil inclinations, a perfect hatred of sin, and a love to Thee above all the desires of this world. Let it be the great employment of our lives to honour and serve Thee, and let our rejoicing be the testimony of our conscience, that in simplicity and godly sincerity, not with fleshly wisdom, but by the grace of God, we live and act in the world.

Our Lord our Keeper, watch over us, and over all who are dear to us, this night. Shield us from all harm; keep us from all sin; and whether we sleep or wake, let us live with Thee. Fulfil Thy promise, that Thou wilt never leave us nor forsake us. Enable us to pass the time of our sojourning in Thy faith, and fear, and love; and when we die, receive us unto Thyself, that we may dwell in Thy presence, and behold Thy face, and sing praises unto Thy name for ever.

[We implore Thy blessing on the children of this family. Teach them to remember Thee in the days of their youth; and keep them by Thy power through faith unto salvation.]

Enable the members of this household, we beseech Thee, to show all fidelity in their appointed duties. And whatsoever they do, dispose them to do it heartily, as unto the Lord and not unto man.

Father of mercies and God of all comfort, look with compassion on the sick and the afflicted. Give them support and comfort in their trials; and overrule Thy fatherly chastening to the everlasting welfare of their souls.

Bless our Queen, our rulers, and our country. Pardon our many national sins; continue to regard us with Thy favour; and make us a people fearing Thee and working righteousness.

Bless Thy whole Church. Unite all Christians in the bonds of a common faith and love, and speedily fill the whole earth with Thy glory.

Give ear, O God, to our humble supplications, for the sake of our only Mediator, Jesus Christ, to whom, with Thee and with the Holy Spirit, be honour and glory for evermore.

OUR Father which art in heaven, Hallowed be Thy name. Thy kingdom come. Thy will be done in earth, as it is in heaven. Give us this day our daily bread. And forgive us our debts, as we forgive our debtors. And lead us not into temptation, but deliver us from evil: For Thine is the kingdom, and the power, and the glory, for ever.—*Amen.*

Saturday Morning.

"I will sing of mercy and judgment: unto Thee, O Lord, will I sing. I will behave myself wisely in a perfect way. O when wilt Thou come unto me? I will walk within my house with a perfect heart."

Let us Pray.

O LORD, open Thou our lips, and our mouth shall show forth Thy praise. Pardon our unworthiness. Help our infirmities, and graciously receive the worship which we render unto Thee, through Christ our Lord. We acknowledge Thee as the Father of lights, from whom cometh down every good and every perfect gift; who forgivest our iniquities, who healest our diseases, who redeemest our life from destruction, who satisfiest our mouth with good things, who crownest us with loving-kindness and tender mercies.

Pardon, O God, our ingratitude for Thy benefits. Fill us with love to Thee, who hast first loved us, and teach us, as becometh the children of so many mercies, to be kind and compassionate towards our fellow-men, loving them out of a pure and fervent heart, and doing them good as we have opportunity.

Above all, give us a deep and abiding sense of the love of Christ, which passeth knowledge; and grant that it may constrain us to walk in love, as Christ also hath loved us. Dispose us to bear one another's burdens, so as to fulfil the law of Christ. Help us to remember the words of the Lord Jesus, that it is more blessed to give than to receive; and make us willing, if need be, to deny ourselves, so that we may more abundantly supply the wants of others. Teach us, as much as lieth in us, to live peaceably with all men, recompensing to no man evil for evil, but overcoming evil with good. Let all bitterness, and wrath, and anger, and clamour, and evil-speaking be put away from us, with all malice; and make us kind, tender-hearted, and forgiving, even as Thou for Christ's sake forgivest us.

We implore Thy blessing on all the members of this family. May they be kindly affectioned one towards another, and find how good and pleasant a thing it is for brethren to dwell together in unity.

We pray for the welfare and happiness of our Sovereign; for the peace and prosperity of our country; for the speedy enlightenment and conversion of all nations.

We beseech Thee to look with compassion on the afflicted, and to grant them all needful relief and consolation.

And now, O God, we commit ourselves to Thee. Watch over us this day; deliver us from all danger; aid us in our lawful occupations; and keep our souls unspotted from the world.

Grant these requests, O Father, we beseech Thee, which we humbly present in the name of Thy beloved Son, our Lord and Saviour.

OUR Father which art in heaven, Hallowed be Thy name. Thy kingdom come. Thy will be done in earth, as it is in heaven. Give us this day our

daily bread. And forgive us our debts, as we forgive our debtors. And lead us not into temptation, but deliver us from evil: For Thine is the kingdom, and the power, and the glory, for ever.—*Amen.*

Saturday Evening.

"If ye then be risen with Christ, seek those things which are above, where Christ sitteth on the right hand of God.

"Set your affection on things above, not on things on the earth."

Let us Pray.

O GOD, of whose grace alone it cometh that we are able to pray to Thee as we ought, deliver us, when we draw nigh to Thee, from wanderings of thought and coldness of affection, and enable us in faith to ask of Thee such things as it shall please Thee to bestow, through the merits of Jesus Christ, our only Mediator.

Pardon, O God, our trespasses and sins, and give us grace, that henceforth we may be enabled to bring forth fruits meet for repentance, and to show our gratitude for Thy goodness by a cheerful and constant obedience to Thy holy will.

Blessed Lord, who hast power to stablish us according to Thy Gospel, strengthen our hearts that we fall not from our steadfastness. Hold Thou us up, and so we shall be safe. Suffer us no more to wander from

Thy ways, or to grow weary in keeping Thy commandments. Whatever of sin or of infirmity Thou seest in us, O Lord, forgive it, and help us to overcome it. Whatever of good Thy grace may have wrought in us, be pleased to confirm and complete it. Make us watchful against temptation; strong in faith; diligent in duty; patient in trial; and fervent in prayer. Teach us to endure hardness as good soldiers of Jesus Christ; and to take unto us the whole armour of God, that we may be able to withstand in the evil day, and having done all to stand.

O Thou that savest by Thy right hand them that put their trust in Thee, grant us defence and deliverance from all the enemies that war against the soul. Let Thy divine power so strengthen our weakness, that neither the craft of the devil, nor the allurements of the world, nor the evil desires of our own hearts, may prevail against us, but that we may in all things be more than conquerors through Him that loved us.

Hear our intercessions, O Lord, in behalf of all our brethren of mankind. We pray for the nations that are sitting in darkness, that it may please Thee to bring them into Thy marvellous light. We pray for Thy Church Universal, and more especially for the Church of our fathers, that truth and godliness may flourish in it more and more, and that its members, united in the bonds of love, may dwell together in unity. We pray for those whom Thou hast visited with affliction, that it may please Thee to comfort and relieve them, and to overrule their trials for the everlasting health and welfare of their souls. We pray for the members of this family, and for all connected with them, that they may be blessed with the joy of Thy salvation, sanctified by the grace of Thy Holy Spirit, and kept by Thy power through faith unto life eternal.

And now, O God, we beseech Thee to watch over us, and over all who are dear to us, this night. Preserve us from all evil; grant us refreshing sleep; and if it please Thee, spare us to enjoy the blessings, and fit us to discharge the duties, of Thy holy day.

These our humble supplications we present in the name and through the mediation of Jesus Christ, our Lord and Saviour.

OUR Father which art in heaven, Hallowed be Thy name. Thy kingdom come. Thy will be done in earth, as it is in heaven. Give us this day our daily bread. And forgive us our debts, as we forgive our debtors. And lead us not into temptation, but deliver us from evil: For Thine is the kingdom, and the power, and the glory, for ever.—*Amen.*

THIRD WEEK.

Lord's Day Morning.

"O give thanks unto the Lord; for He is good: for His mercy endureth for ever."

LET US PRAY.

ALMIGHTY GOD, who hast watched over us during the night, and permitted us to see the light of a new day of rest, grant that through the intercession of Thy well-beloved Son, and the effectual working of Thy Holy Spirit, we may be able to use the privileges of this holy day to Thy glory.

This is the day which the Lord hath made; we will rejoice and be glad in it. Glory be unto Thee, O God, that on the first day of the week Thou didst raise up Thy Son from the dead, and give Him glory, that our faith and hope might be in Thee. Thou art our God, and we will praise Thee; Thou art our God, we will exalt Thee, and praise Thy name for ever.

O our God, we confess our sins to Thee. Our hearts condemn us, and our sins witness against us. We are unable of ourselves to render any acceptable service to Thee. When we would do good, evil is present with us.

O Lord, with whom is forgiveness that Thou mayest be feared, and plenteous redemption; have mercy upon us.

O God, who hast not appointed us to wrath, but to obtain salvation by our Lord Jesus Christ; have mercy upon us.

Remember not against us former transgressions; but, in Thy mercy, pardon us, for Thy goodness' sake, O Lord. Justify us freely by Thy grace through the redemption that is in Christ Jesus, and give us the peace that passeth understanding.

Father of mercies, receive our humble and hearty thanks for all Thy goodness. We bless Thy name, that Thou hast bountifully provided for us not only such things as are serviceable for the body, but such also as are needful for the soul. We thank Thee for the holy rest of Thy day, for the instructions of Thy Word, for the ordinances of Thy worship, for the promised grace of Thy Holy Spirit, and, above all, for Jesus Christ, Thine unspeakable gift, in whom Thou hast blessed us with all spiritual and heavenly blessings. Forbid, O God, that the privileges we enjoy should rise up against us to our condemnation. Grant that our profiting by them may appear in a life of obedience to Thy will; and that the services of Thy Church on earth may prepare us for the worship of the Church in heaven.

O Lord, who hast said that where two or three are gathered together in Thy name, there Thou art in the midst of them, be present this day in all assemblies of Thy people. Let Thy Word everywhere have free course and be glorified. Direct, by Thy Spirit, those who shall preach the Gospel of Christ; and open the hearts of Thy people to receive the truth.

Draw nigh to such as are withheld from the public worship of Thy Church; and grant unto them the joy of Thy favour and the comfort of Thy fellowship. Have pity on those who forsake Thine ordinances, and bring them to repentance. Increase everywhere the number of Thy true worshippers; and hasten the time when, throughout the whole world, Thy name shall be honoured, and Thy Word believed.

Incline Thine ear, O God, to our supplications, which we offer in the name of Thy beloved Son, our Lord and Saviour.

OUR Father which art in heaven, Hallowed be Thy name. Thy kingdom come. Thy will be done in earth, as it is in heaven. Give us this day our daily bread. And forgive us our debts, as we forgive our debtors. And lead us not into temptation, but deliver us from evil: For Thine is the kingdom, and the power, and the glory, for ever.—*Amen.*

Lord's Day Evening.

"If my people, which are called by my name, shall humble themselves, and pray, and seek my face, and turn from their wicked ways; then will I hear from heaven, and will forgive their sin, and will heal their land."

Let us Pray.

ALMIGHTY GOD, who hast given us all things that pertain unto life and godliness, we thank Thee for another day of the Son of man, and for renewed opportunities of hearing Thy Word and showing forth Thy praise.

Pardon, O Lord, the sins and errors of our holy services. Enter not into judgment with us for the weakness of our faith, the dulness of our hope, and the coldness of our love; but of Thy great mercy accept our worship, for the sake of Jesus Christ our great High Priest and Mediator.

Let it please Thee also to bless for our edification those lessons of divine truth which we have this day heard. Suffer not the good seed to be caught away, by the wicked one, out of our hearts; but cause it to take such root within us, that it may bring forth fruit abundantly to Thy praise.

We confess that we have often been unprofitable hearers of Thy Word. Pardon this sin, O Lord. Give us grace, that henceforth we may be enabled more faithfully to receive Thy Gospel, that we may be made wise unto salvation, thoroughly furnished unto all good works; and enable us, by the grace of Thy Holy Spirit, to walk more and more in accordance with its precepts.

Bless Thy whole Church; heal its divisions; purify it from error and corruption; and grant that all its members may be united in the belief and love of the truth.

Graciously hear us, O God, while we plead with

Thee for our fellow-men. Open, we beseech Thee, a great and effectual door for the preaching of Thy blessed Gospel everywhere. Remove the veil from the hearts of Thine ancient people; dispel the darkness and superstition of the heathen; and hasten the time when all the ends of the earth shall turn to Thee, and all the kindreds of the nations shall worship before Thee.

Bestow Thy special blessing on our Sovereign the Queen, the Prince and Princess of Wales, and all the other members of the Royal Family. Give them grace that they may adorn their high station; and make them signal instruments to advance Thy glory and the public good.

Incline the hearts of Christian parents to bring up their children in the nurture and admonition of the Lord; that they may be prepared rightly to fulfil their several callings in this life, and in the life to come may inherit Thy heavenly kingdom.

[Bless the children of this family. Keep them from the evil that is in the world, and cause them to grow in knowledge and in grace. Bless the servants in this household, and enable them in all things to serve the Lord Christ, our Master in heaven.]

Give to all Thine afflicted people the supports and consolations of Thy grace. Relieve the sick. Comfort the sorrowful. Supply the wants of the needy. Dispel the fears of the dying, and prepare them for their change.

Be gracious to all of us according to our need. Take us this night under Thy protection. Fulfil to us Thy promise, that Thou wilt never leave nor forsake Thy people. Guide us by Thy counsel while we live, and afterward receive us into glory, through Jesus Christ, in whose name we present our prayers.

OUR Father which art in heaven, Hallowed be Thy name. Thy kingdom come. Thy will be done in earth, as it is in heaven. Give us this day our daily bread. And forgive us our debts, as we forgive our debtors. And lead us not into temptation, but deliver us from evil: For Thine is the kingdom, and the power, and the glory, for ever.—*Amen.*

Monday Morning.

" O God, Thou art my God; early will I seek Thee."

LET US PRAY.

FATHER of mercies, who hast refreshed us by Thy day of rest and the sleep of the past night, and art now calling us to go forth to our work and to our labour until evening, we praise Thee for Thy goodness, and ask the continuance of Thy favour, for Jesus' sake.

Give us grace, that we may walk worthy of Thee in the concerns and business of our daily life, and grant that, throughout this week, the influence of Thy Word and worship may be upon us. Keep us mindful that Thou art calling us to serve Thee in whatsoever place Thy providence hath assigned to us. And make us faithful in that which is least, as well as in that which is greatest.

Forgive, O Lord, our proneness to forget Thee amidst the pursuits and engagements of the world. Strengthen us to withstand temptation; guard us against the deceitfulness of our own hearts; and enable us, by the grace of Thy Holy Spirit, to acknowledge Thee in all our ways.

Let Thy presence go with us this day. Enable us to be honest in the discharge of every trust, diligent in duty, patient in trial, and steadfast in the resistance of temptation. Enable us in all things to live to Thy glory, and to use every opportunity of doing good. As we live by Thy mercy, may we live to Thy praise. Whatsoever our hand findeth to do, may we do it with our might, remembering that there is no work, nor device, nor knowledge, nor wisdom, in the grave, whither we are going.

Be gracious to our relatives and friends. Remember them for good, and visit them with Thy salvation.

Comfort the afflicted. Provide for the poor. Reclaim the erring. Enlighten those who are perishing for lack of knowledge; and speedily diffuse Thy Gospel throughout the world.

Graciously hear us, O God, and have mercy upon us, through Jesus Christ, our Saviour.

OUR Father which art in heaven, Hallowed be Thy name. Thy kingdom come. Thy will be done in earth, as it is in heaven. Give us this day our daily bread. And forgive us our debts, as we forgive our debtors. And lead us not into temptation, but deliver us from evil: For Thine is the kingdom, and the power, and the glory, for ever.—*Amen.*

Monday Evening.

"Thou makest the outgoings of the morning and evening to rejoice."

Let us Pray.

O THOU that hearest prayer, unto Thee shall all flesh come. Bow down Thine ear, O Lord; hear us, for we are poor and needy. Rejoice the souls of Thy servants, for unto Thee do we lift up our souls; for Thou, Lord, art good, and ready to forgive, and plenteous in mercy unto all them that call upon Thee.

O Thou Holy One, with whom evil cannot dwell, we acknowledge and confess before Thee the manifold sins, which in thought, word, and deed, we have committed against Thee. All we like sheep have gone astray; we have turned every one to his own way. We have followed the devices and desires of our own hearts. We have often slighted Thy counsels, abused Thy mercies, distrusted Thy promises, and broken Thy commandments.

Enter not, O Lord, into judgment with Thy servants, for in Thy sight shall no man living be justified. But let it please Thee, through the merits of Thy beloved Son, to receive us graciously and love us freely.

Gracious God, who desirest not sacrifice, and hast no delight in burnt-offering, but who dost not despise a broken and contrite heart, pour out upon us the grace of Thy Holy Spirit, that we may be sorry for our sins against Thee. Grant that our sorrow may be of that godly sort, which worketh repentance unto salvation not to be repented of. Save us from deceiving ourselves by confessing and lamenting our sins while we yet cleave to them. Enable us to bring forth fruits meet for repentance. Dispose us to hate and shun every false way, to mortify all sinful inclinations, to resist and subdue all evil habits, and to be ready to do every good work.

Forasmuch as Thou knowest with how many and how great temptations we are encompassed on every side, and how unable we are to withstand them in our own strength, we pray Thee to uphold us by Thy might, and to make Thy grace sufficient for us, so that we may in all things be more than conquerors, and may in the end obtain the inheritance which Thou hast promised to him that overcometh.

Hear our intercessions, O God, on behalf of those whom Thou hast afflicted. Grant them support and comfort in their trials. May Thy chastening, though for the present grievous, afterward yield in them the peaceable fruits of righteousness.

We commend to Thee all those who are in sorrow for their sins. May Thy Holy Spirit work in them true repentance, and lead them to Jesus Christ their Lord, that by faith they may obtain holiness unto life eternal. Visit them with the joy of Thy salvation, and uphold them with Thy free Spirit.

We pray for the scornful and the thoughtless, that it may please Thee to awaken and convert them, and to bring them to the knowledge and obedience of Thy Gospel.

Look with compassion, we beseech Thee, on the whole world. Hasten the time when repentance and remission of sins shall be preached in the name of Jesus to all nations, and when men everywhere shall be blessed in Him and shall call Him blessed.

O Thou keeper of Israel, watch over us, and over all who are near and dear to us, this night. Shield us from danger. Grant us, if it please Thee, quiet and refreshing sleep, and bring us in safety to the light of another day.

Hear us, O God, and grant an answer of peace, through Jesus Christ, our Saviour.

OUR Father which art in heaven, Hallowed be Thy name. Thy kingdom come. Thy will be done in earth, as it is in heaven. Give us this day our daily bread. And forgive us our debts, as we forgive our debtors. And lead us not into temptation, but deliver us from evil: For Thine is the kingdom, and the power, and the glory, for ever.—*Amen.*

Tuesday Morning.

"O how love I Thy law! it is my meditation all the day."

Let us Pray.

O GOD, who dwellest in the heavens, but who hast revealed Thyself to men in Thy Word and in Thy works, enable us, we beseech Thee, through Jesus

Christ our Lord, to come unto Thee by faith, believing that Thou art our Father and our God, and a rewarder of them that diligently seek Thee.

Pardon, for the sake of Thy beloved Son, our lack of faith; and teach us to trust Thee with all our heart. Help us so to set Thee always before us, that, amidst all adversities and trials, we may steadfastly endure, as seeing Thee who art invisible. Dispose us to cast upon Thee all our care, and to look to Thee for the supply of all our need, in the full assurance that Thou carest for us and wilt not withhold from us any good thing. Above all, teach us unfeignedly to rest on the merits and grace of Thine only-begotten Son, who bore our sins in His own body on the tree, and who ever liveth to make intercession for us. And forasmuch as Thou hast given us in Thy Word many promises concerning eternal life, grant that we, being persuaded of them and embracing them, may confess that we are strangers and pilgrims on the earth, desiring a better country, that is an heavenly. Increase our faith, O God, and by the power of Thy Holy Spirit enable us to bear patiently every sorrow, to discharge faithfully every duty, and to resist firmly every temptation, while we look, not at the things which are seen and temporal, but at the things which are unseen and eternal.

Be Thou, O Lord, our protection, who art our redemption; direct our minds by Thy gracious presence, and watch over our paths with guiding love, that among the snares which lie hidden in this path wherein we walk, we may so pass onward with hearts fixed on Thee, that by the track of faith, we may come to where Thou wouldest have us.

Impart the like precious faith to our beloved friends. Increase everywhere the number of Thy faithful people. Encourage all who are in trouble or affliction to put their trust under the shadow of Thy wings. And let it be the comfort of the dying to know that their Redeemer liveth, and that because He liveth they shall live also.

Grant to us this day Thy favour and protection. Shield us from evil; keep us from sin; and enable us to pass the time of our sojourning here in Thy fear, looking for the blessed hope and appearing of the glory of our great Lord and Saviour, Jesus Christ.

OUR Father which art in heaven, Hallowed be Thy name. Thy kingdom come. Thy will be done in earth, as it is in heaven. Give us this day our daily bread. And forgive us our debts, as we forgive our debtors. And lead us not into temptation, but deliver us from evil: For Thine is the kingdom, and the power, and the glory, for ever.—*Amen.*

Tuesday Evening.

"Behold, the eye of the Lord is upon them that fear Him, upon them that hope in His mercy.

"Our soul waiteth for the Lord: He is our help and our shield."

Let us Pray.

ALMIGHTY GOD, who hast given us in Christ Jesus exceeding great and precious promises, both for the life that now is and for that which is to come, enable us to set our hope in Thee. Remember Thy Word unto Thy servants, upon which Thou hast caused us to hope; and of Thy great mercy in Jesus Christ, pardon our sins, and by Thy Holy Spirit fill us with all joy and peace in believing.

O God, who hast assured us in Thy Word, that in due season we shall reap if we faint not, suffer us not to grow weary in welldoing; but grant that, encouraged by Thy promises, we may be able both to do and to suffer Thy holy will in all things. Strengthen us to bear all our trials and afflictions, reckoning that the sufferings of this present time are not worthy to be compared with the glory which shall be revealed in us.

Give us grace, whereby we may be enabled to hold fast the confidence and rejoicing of our hope firm unto the end. Amidst the storms of adversity let this hope be to us an anchor of the soul, both sure and steadfast. And when the time of our departure comes, grant that we may be able to commit the keeping of our souls unto Thee, in sure and certain hope of that eternal life which Thou hast promised through Jesus Christ, our Saviour.

Hear our intercessions, we beseech Thee, for those whom we ought to remember in our prayers.

[We commend to Thy care our relatives and friends. Bless the children of this family. May they be children of Thy kingdom, remembering their Creator in the days of their youth. Be gracious to the servants of this household. Enable them to show all good fidelity in their appointed station; and whatsoever they do, dispose them to do it heartily, as unto the Lord, and not unto men.]

And now, O God, we beseech Thee to watch over

us this night. Suffer no evil to befall us, nor any plague to come nigh our dwelling; and, if it please Thee, raise us on the morrow to enjoy the blessings and discharge the duties of another day.

These our humble supplications we present in the name and through the mediation of Jesus Christ, our Lord and Saviour.

OUR Father which art in heaven, Hallowed be Thy name. Thy kingdom come. Thy will be done in earth, as it is in heaven. Give us this day our daily bread. And forgive us our debts, as we forgive our debtors. And lead us not into temptation, but deliver us from evil: For Thine is the kingdom, and the power, and the glory, for ever.—*Amen.*

Wednesday Morning.

"Lord, Thou hast been our dwelling place in all generations. Before the mountains were brought forth, or ever Thou hadst formed the earth and the world, even from everlasting to everlasting, Thou art God."

LET US PRAY.

O GOD, who art very pitiful and of tender mercy; who regardest the poor, and art kind to the unthankful and the evil, dispose us heartily to acknowledge Thy goodness, and trustfully to commit ourselves to Thy care.

Enter not into judgment with us for the shortcomings and sins whereby we have provoked Thee. For Christ's sake forgive us. Continue to us, notwithstanding our unworthiness, the bounties of Thy providence and the riches of Thy grace; and teach us to show our gratitude for Thy benefits, by cheerful obedience to Thy holy will.

Help us to live in charity with all men, seeking to bear their burdens, ministering to their wants, pitying their distresses, forgiving their provocations, and doing them good as we have opportunity.

Specially we pray that our love may be increased toward those that are of the household of faith. Teach us to delight in them as the excellent of the earth; to deal kindly with them, because Thou hast a favour to them; to honour them as those whom the Saviour loves, and whom He requires us to love for His sake.

Graciously hear us, O God, while we plead with Thee for all whom we ought to remember at the throne of grace. Bless our friends; reward our benefactors; forgive our enemies, and enable us from the heart to forgive them.

May it please Thee to provide for the necessities of the poor; to relieve and comfort the afflicted; and to incline those that are rich in this world to be ready to distribute and willing to communicate.

Regard the young with Thy favour; and satisfy them early with Thy mercy, that they may rejoice and be glad all their days.

Sustain those who are bowed down with age and infirmity.

Unite all Christians in the bonds of a common

faith, and dispose them to love one another out of a pure heart fervently.

Have mercy on all men. Reclaim them from their errors. Save them from their miseries. Cleanse them from their sins; and bring them to the faith and obedience of Thy Gospel.

May the power of Thy Holy Spirit work throughout all the world, enlightening, sanctifying, and comforting all believers, and inciting them to make known the glad tidings of salvation to others as Thou givest them opportunity.

And now, O our God, we commit ourselves to Thee. Aid us this day in our several occupations. Teach us, in our intercourse with our fellow-men, to walk in love as Christ also hath loved us. And whatsoever we would that men should do unto us, help us to do even so to them.

Grant these requests, O Father, we beseech Thee, and all other things which Thou knowest to be needful for us, through Jesus Christ, our Saviour.

OUR Father which art in heaven, Hallowed be Thy name. Thy kingdom come. Thy will be done in earth, as it is in heaven. Give us this day our daily bread. And forgive us our debts, as we forgive our debtors. And lead us not into temptation, but deliver us from evil: For Thine is the kingdom, and the power, and the glory, for ever.—*Amen.*

Wednesday Evening.

"God is my King of old, working salvation in the midst of the earth.

"The day is Thine, the night also is Thine: Thou hast prepared the light and the sun."

LET US PRAY.

ALMIGHTY GOD, in whom alone is rest, incline Thine ear to our prayers, and grant us an answer of peace. For the sake of Him, on whom was laid the chastisement of our peace, show Thy mercy upon us, and grant that we may be reconciled unto Thee. Enable us to flee for refuge to the hope set before us in the Gospel, that, being justified by faith, we may have peace with Thee through our Lord Jesus Christ, and may ever joy in Thee through Him by whom we have received the atonement.

Lead us by Thy Holy Spirit, to walk in the ways of Thy commandments, and cause us to delight in them as ways of pleasantness and paths of peace. Deliver us from the anxious cares, the unruly passions, and the covetous affections, whereby men's hearts are disquieted within them.

O God our heavenly Father, who hast promised that Thou wilt keep him in perfect peace whose mind is stayed on Thee, grant unto us, for the sake of the Lord Jesus Christ, a perfect confidence in Thy power and love, that we may be possessors of the heavenly peace.

Take away, we beseech Thee, sin which is enmity to Thee, and the doubts which disturb our minds. Fill our hearts with the very Spirit of Christ, Himself our righteousness, and Prince of Peace. Give us in rich measure Thy Holy Spirit, that we may evermore rest in the joy of Thy heavenly love.

O God, we humbly commit ourselves, and all whom we love, to Thy fatherly protection. Pardon the sins of the past day, and give us grace that we may heartily repent of them. Give us quiet sleep this night, and grant that on the morrow we may awake refreshed, ready for the duties of another day.

Comfort, we pray Thee, all who are in adversity or affliction. Give the joy of Thy salvation to those who for their sins are in bitterness of spirit. Speak peace to them that are afar off, and bring them nigh, through the blood of Christ.

Grant, O Lord, that this family, devoted to Thy service, and confiding in Thy protection, may obtain the blessing which they humbly implore; that being at rest under Thy defence, they may not be left destitute of assistance for this life, and may be prepared for the good things which are eternal, through Jesus Christ our Lord.

Graciously answer our prayers, O God, and let Thy peace, which passeth all understanding, keep our hearts and minds, through Jesus Christ; to whom, with Thee and with the Holy Spirit, be glory everlasting.

OUR Father which art in heaven, Hallowed be Thy name. Thy kingdom come. Thy will be done in earth, as it is in heaven. Give us this day our daily bread. And forgive us our debts, as we forgive our debtors. And lead us not into temptation, but deliver us from evil: For Thine is the kingdom, and the power, and the glory, for ever.—*Amen.*

Thursday Morning.

"Blessed be God, which hath not turned away my prayer, nor His mercy from me."

LET US PRAY.

ALMIGHTY GOD, who hast caused the light of another day to shine upon us, we give Thee thanks for that better light of Thy glorious Gospel, wherewith Thou hast visited us.

Help us, we beseech Thee, as children of the light and of the day, to renounce the hidden things of dishonesty, and to have no fellowship with the unfruitful works of darkness. And enable us, by Thy Holy Spirit, to adorn the doctrine of God our Saviour, and to be faithful followers of Thy Son, whom Thou hast sent to be the Light of the world.

O God, who hast not appointed us to wrath, but to obtain salvation by our Lord Jesus Christ, who died for us, that, whether we wake or sleep, we should live together with Him; give us grace that, conformed to His image on earth, we may be prepared for dwelling with Him in heaven, where we shall be like Him, for we shall see Him as He is. Make us willing to take His yoke upon us, and to learn of Him who was meek and lowly in heart. Teach us, after His example, to walk in love; to go about doing good; to bear patiently all evil treatment, and to do Thy will and finish the work Thou hast given us to do.

Pardon, O Lord, our manifold shortcomings in these things during the time that is past. Give us, O God, Thy heavenly grace, that we all, with open face, beholding as in a glass the glory of the Lord, may be changed into the same image from glory to glory, even as by the Spirit of the Lord. Grant that we may all come in the unity of the faith and of the knowledge of the Son of God, unto a perfect man, unto the measure of the stature of the fulness of Christ.

Graciously hear us, O God, while we plead with Thee, not for ourselves only, but also for our brethren of mankind. Our heart's desire and prayer is, that they may be saved. Bring all such as are in unbelief or error to a saving knowledge of Jesus Christ. We pray for all, that the mind which was in Christ Jesus may be found also in them. Specially give unto Thy servants who are afflicted, a spirit of submission to Thy holy will, enabling them patiently to bear their cross and to follow Christ.

[Bestow Thy blessing on the children of this family, and cause them to grow in grace as they grow in years. Regard with favour the servants of this house, and enable them, in their appointed station, faithfully to serve and honour Thee, their Master in heaven.]

And now, O our God, we humbly commit ourselves, and all whom we love, to Thy guidance and protection. Shield us from danger; keep us from sin. Aid us in our lawful occupations. And whatsoever we do, in word or deed, dispose us to do all in the name of the

Lord Jesus, through whom we humbly offer our supplications, and to whom, with Thee and with the Holy Spirit, be glory everlasting.

OUR Father which art in heaven, Hallowed be Thy name. Thy kingdom come. Thy will be done in earth, as it is in heaven. Give us this day our daily bread. And forgive us our debts, as we forgive our debtors. And lead us not into temptation, but deliver us from evil: For Thine is the kingdom, and the power, and the glory, for ever.—*Amen.*

Thursday Evening

"The sacrifices of God are a broken spirit: a broken and a contrite heart, O God, Thou wilt not despise."

Let us Pray.

ALMIGHTY GOD, who knowest all things, and who searchest the hearts of the children of men, we humble ourselves before Thee this evening, under a deep sense of our unworthiness, and earnestly seek Thy mercy to forgive us our sins, and Thy grace to cleanse us from them.

Pardon, we beseech Thee, for the sake of Thy beloved Son, whatever evil we have done, or said, or thought this day, and enable us, for the time to come, to be watchful lest in anything we offend against Thee.

Lead us by Thy Holy Spirit to Jesus Christ our Saviour, and sanctify us by His grace that we may ever obey Thy law.

Teach us to deny ourselves, and to take up our cross daily, as faithful followers of Thy dear Son. Make us willing, after His example, that Thy will, and not our own, be done; and strengthen us to endure affliction for His sake. Teach us so to control our affections, and to use a wise abstinence even from things lawful, that earthly things may not obtain dominion over us. Grant that through faith we may be able to lay aside every weight, and the sin which doth so easily beset us, and to run with patience the race that is set before us, looking unto Jesus, the Author and Finisher of our Faith, who, for the joy that was set before Him, endured the cross, despising the shame, and is set down at the right hand of the throne of God.

Father of mercies, we give Thee hearty thanks for the goodness Thou hast this day bestowed upon us; and we humbly commit ourselves, and all whom we love, to Thy fatherly care this night. Keep us, O God, during the night watches, and bring us in safety to the morning hours.

Seeing that Thou, O Lord, hast ordained that men should dwell together in families, be pleased so to order all things in this, and all families of Thy people, that in every household Thy name may be hallowed and Thy law obeyed.

We pray for our relatives and friends, that it may please Thee to remember them with the favour that Thou bearest unto Thy people, and to visit them with Thy salvation.

Give Thy grace to parents and children, and to

masters and servants, that they may rightly perform their duties as seeing Thee, the Father of all, and knowing that one is their Master, even Christ.

We pray for the sick, the sorrowful, and the dying, that it may please Thee to comfort and support them, and to grant them a happy deliverance out of all their troubles.

Bless and long preserve our gracious Sovereign. Extend Thy favour and protection to our country. Give peace and welfare to the nations, and hasten the time when all the kingdoms of the world shall become the kingdom of our Lord and of His Christ.

For Thy great mercy's sake, O God, grant us an answer to these our prayers, which we offer in the name of Thy well-beloved Son, to whom, with Thee and with the Holy Spirit, be glory everlasting.

OUR Father which art in heaven, Hallowed be Thy name. Thy kingdom come. Thy will be done in earth, as it is in heaven. Give us this day our daily bread. And forgive us our debts, as we forgive our debtors. And lead us not into temptation, but deliver us from evil: For Thine is the kingdom, and the power, and the glory, for ever.—*Amen.*

Friday Morning.

"O Lord, open Thou my lips; and my mouth shall show forth Thy praise."

Let us Pray.

ALMIGHTY GOD, the source of all goodness, who art always more ready to hear than we are to pray, and art able to do for us above all that we ask or think; we cast ourselves on Thy fatherly care, and humbly ask Thee for Christ's sake to supply our need.

We confess, O God, that we know not what things are best for us. Give us faith in Thy wisdom and goodness. Feed us with food convenient for us. Bless us with health of body and soundness of mind. Endue us with knowledge and prudence, and direct us in all our labours. Further our lawful undertakings with Thy help and blessing, and grant us such success as seemeth good in Thy sight.

O most merciful Father, we leave all our concerns at Thy disposal. Give us grace to believe, that as Thou didst not spare thine own Son, but didst deliver Him up for us all, it is Thy will also freely to give us all things. Confirm our trust in Thy promise that they who seek Thee shall not lack any good thing; and as we pass on our way, sustain and comfort us by the hope of the glorious inheritance which Thou art reserving for Thy children.

Jesus our Master, do Thou meet us while we walk in the way, and long to reach the heavenly country; so that, following Thy light, we may keep the way of righteousness, and never wander into the darkness of this world's night, whilst Thou, who art the Way, the Truth, and the Life, art striving within us.

Father of mercies, we give Thee hearty thanks for all the benefits which it hath pleased Thee hitherto to bestow upon us. Pardon, for Christ's sake, wherein we have offended Thee by forgetting or abusing them, and enable us henceforth, by the grace of Thy Holy Spirit, to acknowledge Thy gifts, and to use them for Thy glory.

[O God, our Creator and Preserver, who givest food to all, causing the grass to grow for the cattle and herb for the service of man, regard our land, we beseech Thee, with Thy mercy, and bless us with favourable weather and fruitful seasons, that our garners may be filled with all manner of store, and our souls may have cause to rejoice in Thy bounty.]

We pray for our fellow-men, that it may please Thee to supply all their need according to Thy riches in glory by Christ Jesus. Provide for the poor; instruct the ignorant; reclaim the erring; comfort the sorrowful; relieve the sick; support the dying, and prepare them for their change. Enlighten the world with the glory of Christ; give to all Christian people grace that they may shine as lights; and hasten the time, O Lord, when holiness shall be the joy of the whole earth.

Grant this for Jesus' sake, O God!

OUR Father which art in heaven, Hallowed be Thy name. Thy kingdom come. Thy will be done in earth, as it is in heaven. Give us this day our daily bread. And forgive us our debts, as we forgive our debtors. And lead us not into temptation, but deliver us from evil: For Thine is the kingdom, and the power, and the glory, for ever.—*Amen.*

Friday Evening.

"Bless the Lord, O my soul: and all that is within me, bless His holy name."

LET US PRAY

O GOD, who by Thy providence hast guided us throughout the past day, and hast brought us in the enjoyment of many mercies to its close, we lift up our souls to Thee, in hearty acknowledgment of Thy goodness.

We confess that we are not worthy of the least of these blessings. And we beseech Thee, for Thy dear Son's sake, to pardon all the ingratitude and forgetfulness, whereby we have provoked Thee to withdraw Thy tender mercies from us. Give us grace also, that we may be enabled more worthily to requite Thy benefits, by heartily loving Thee, confidently trusting in Thee, and cheerfully yielding up ourselves to Thy service.

We thank Thee for the preservation of our lives, and the supply of our wants; for health of body and soundness of mind; and for strength and skill to labour.

We thank Thee for any success that has crowned our labours, and for the portion of earthly good which Thou hast bestowed upon us.

We thank Thee for the fellowship and sympathy of kindred and friends.

We thank Thee for the goodly land of light, and peace, and liberty, in which Thou hast cast our lot; and for all our temporal comforts and enjoyments.

We give thanks unto Thee, O God, for Thou art good, for Thy mercy endureth for ever.

Above all, we magnify Thy name for Thy great mercy to our souls. We thank Thee that Thou hast so loved us, as to give Thine only-begotten Son for our redemption.

We thank Thee for the gift of the Holy Spirit; and for Thy Holy Word, which is able to make us wise unto salvation.

We thank Thee for all spiritual influences, for the power of conscience, and the knowledge of the truth.

We thank Thee for the gifts of faith and hope and charity; and for the promise of everlasting life.

We thank Thee for whatever power these gifts of Thine have given us to do right, and for the comfort which the knowledge of all Thy goodness has brought into our lives.

We give thanks unto Thee, O God, for Thou art good, and Thy mercy in Christ Jesus endureth for ever.

We pray for our fellow-creatures, that it may please Thee to succour and relieve them according to their necessities. Have mercy on those who are sitting in darkness, and bring them to the knowledge and obedience of Thy truth. Look down in pity on the sick, the destitute, the sorrowful, and the dying. Give them support and comfort in their affliction, and in Thy good time deliverance out of all their troubles.

Merciful Father, who givest Thy beloved sleep,

give us rest this night; and if it please Thee, spare us again to see the morning light, and on the morrow send us forth refreshed, to render unto Thee glad and faithful service.

Graciously hear us, for the sake of Thy beloved Son, to whom, with Thee and with the Holy Spirit, be honour and glory, world without end.

OUR Father which art in heaven, Hallowed be Thy name. Thy kingdom come. Thy will be done in earth, as it is in heaven. Give us this day our daily bread. And forgive us our debts, as we forgive our debtors. And lead us not into temptation, but deliver us from evil: For Thine is the kingdom, and the power, and the glory, for ever.—*Amen.*

Saturday Morning.

"O Thou that hearest prayer, unto Thee shall all flesh come."

Let us Pray.

O GOD, who hast taught us to ask, and we shall receive; to seek, and we shall find; and to knock, and it shall be opened unto us; incline Thine ear, we beseech Thee, to our supplications; and enable us, with the confidence of Thy children, to utter before Thee the desires of our hearts.

We are unworthy, O Lord, that Thou shouldst regard us, but in the name of Jesus, Thy beloved Son, we approach Thy throne of grace. For His sake, pardon our sins, purify our hearts, help our infirmities, and work in us that which is well-pleasing in Thy sight.

Almighty God, who by Thy wise decree hast ordered our lot, and determined the bounds of our habitation, help us to occupy contentedly and faithfully our appointed place in life. Fit us for the discharge of its duties. Strengthen us for the endurance of its trials. Guard us against its dangers and temptations. Dispose us to improve the opportunities it affords of glorifying Thee, and of doing good to our fellow-men.

Suffer us not to walk disorderly, but grant that we may be able, at all times, to be quiet, and to do our own business, and to work with our own hands, as Thou hast appointed us.

Enable us to render unto all their dues; fear to whom fear, honour to whom honour, tribute to whom tribute, service to whom service is due; exercising ourselves to have always a conscience void of offence toward Thee and toward men.

Give us grace, O God, as we pass through the world, not to mind earthly things, but to love things heavenly; and even now, while we are placed among things that are passing away, to cleave to those that shall abide, through Jesus Christ our Lord.

Keep all the members of this household in Thy fear and love. Give grace to all. Make us kindly affectioned one to another; and enable us to show how good and pleasant it is for brethren to dwell together in unity. Bless us as we go forth to the labours of the day, and guide us therein by Thy Holy Spirit, that we may do all things to Thy glory.

Bless our Sovereign, and all in authority over us, and enable them to rule in Thy fear. Bless all ranks and conditions of men throughout the land. Help them, in their stations, faithfully to walk with Thee. Give prosperity and peace to our native land, and cause the glory of the Lord Jesus Christ to shine upon all nations.

Stir up Thy Church in all its branches to labour and pray for the conversion of the world to Christ and His service. Father of mercies, have pity on the afflicted. Enable them to glorify Thee by submission to Thy will; and let Thy chastening, though for the present not joyous but grievous, yield in them afterward the peaceable fruits of righteousness.

Graciously hear us, O God, and have mercy on us, through Jesus Christ, our Saviour.

OUR Father which art in heaven, Hallowed be Thy name. Thy kingdom come. Thy will be done in earth, as it is in heaven. Give us this day our daily bread. And forgive us our debts, as we forgive our debtors. And lead us not into temptation, but deliver us from evil: For Thine is the kingdom, and the power, and the glory, for ever.—*Amen.*

Saturday Evening.

"The Lord will command His loving-kindness in the daytime, and in the night His song shall be with me, and my prayer unto the God of my life."

Let us Pray.

ALMIGHTY GOD, our heavenly Father, we bless Thee that, by Thy mercy, we have been brought in safety to the close of another week. We thank Thee for Thy mercy, and for the good hope we have of enjoying on the morrow the rest and privileges of Thy holy day.

Teach us, by Thy Holy Spirit, while we use our sacred privileges on earth, to remember that they are given to prepare us for a higher life.

O God, we thank Thee for the assurance Thou hast given us, that if our earthly house of this tabernacle were dissolved, we have a building of God, an house not made with hands, eternal in the heavens.

Forbid that our hearts should at any time be overcharged with the cares, and riches, and pleasures of this life. Let it be our chief concern to lay up treasure in heaven. Vouchsafe to us, through Thy Spirit, such foretaste of the promised bliss as shall cause us to esteem all earthly joy as vanity, and lead us ever onward in Thy ways, until we appear before Thee in the heavenly Zion.

To Thy care, O God, we commend ourselves this night. Shield us from all evil. Grant us rest. And wake us on the morrow, with hearts disposed to enjoy the privileges and discharge the duties of Thy Sabbath.

We pray for the members of this family, and for all who by the ties of kindred are connected with us, that they may be blessed with Thy favour, which is better than life.

We pray for all those in adversity and affliction, that it may please Thee to succour and relieve them according to their necessities. Be a father of the fatherless, and a judge of the widows, a friend to the stranger, and a refuge for the helpless. Relieve the sick. Comfort the sorrowful. Have mercy on those who are drawing near to death. Let Thy presence sustain them, when flesh and heart are failing.

We pray for the whole human race, and that it may please Thee to make Thy way known upon earth, and Thy saving health among all nations. Pour out Thy Spirit upon all flesh. Turn men everywhere from darkness unto light, and from the power of Satan unto Thee, that they may receive forgiveness of their sins, and inheritance among them that are sanctified.

Give ear, we pray Thee, to our humble supplications, which we offer in the name of Thine only-begotten Son, our Lord and Saviour.

OUR Father which art in heaven, Hallowed be Thy name. Thy kingdom come. Thy will be done in earth, as it is in heaven. Give us this day our daily bread. And forgive us our debts, as we forgive our debtors. And lead us not into temptation, but deliver us from evil: For Thine is the kingdom, and the power, and the glory, for ever.—*Amen.*

FOURTH WEEK.

Lord's Day Morning.

"Moreover also I gave them my Sabbaths, to be a sign between me and them, that they might know that I am the Lord that sanctify them."

LET US PRAY.

O THOU that dwellest in the heavens, unto Thee do we lift up our souls. Dispose us, on this day of rest, which Thou hast hallowed, to give Thee the glory due unto Thy name, and to worship Thee in the beauty of holiness. And seeing we have a great High Priest, who is touched with the feeling of our infirmities, and who ever liveth to make intercession for us, enable us through Him to come boldly unto the throne of grace, that we may obtain mercy, and find grace to help in time of need.

Thou art worthy, O Lord, to receive glory, and honour, and power; for Thou hast created all things, and for Thy pleasure they are and were created. Great and marvellous are Thy works, Lord God Almighty; just and true are Thy ways, Thou King of saints. Who shall not fear Thee, O Lord, and glorify Thy name? for Thou only art holy.

We have broken Thy holy laws, times and ways without number. We have been unthankful for Thy benefits. We have slighted the calls and promises of Thy Word. We have turned a deaf ear to Thy warnings and admonitions.

Almighty God, Father of our Lord Jesus Christ, who desirest not the death of a sinner, but rather that he should turn from his wickedness and live, have mercy on us according to Thy loving-kindness, and according to the multitude of Thy tender mercies blot out our transgressions.

O Son of God, Redeemer of the world, who hast loved us, and given Thyself for us, show us Thy mercy, and grant us Thy salvation. Wash us from our sins in Thy precious blood, and through Thine intercession save us to the uttermost.

O blessed Spirit, the Comforter and Sanctifier, let Thy grace be shed abroad in our hearts. Convince us of sin, and bring us to repentance. Enlighten our minds in the knowledge of Thy truth. And enable us so to receive those gracious promises which are given us in Christ Jesus, that we may be filled with all joy and peace in believing, and may abound in hope through the power of the Holy Spirit.

O Lord of Hosts, of whose glory the whole earth is full, enable us to glorify Thee in our body and in our spirit, which are Thine.

Vouchsafe Thy presence this day in all worshipping assemblies of Thy people; and enable Thy ministering servants faithfully and earnestly to declare Thy blessed Word. Give success to all missionaries of the Cross. May Thy kingdom come, over all the world.

Draw near to such as are necessarily withheld from worshipping in Thy courts. Hear Thou their prayers, and give them the consolations of Thy grace.

Have pity on those who are wandering in error, or sitting in darkness, or hardening themselves in sin. Cause Thy marvellous light to shine upon them, and grant them repentance unto life.

Give to all the faithful the good gifts of the Holy Spirit, that they may grow in grace and in the knowledge of their Lord and Saviour Jesus Christ, looking for and earnestly desiring the coming of the day of God.

Graciously hear us, O God, and have mercy upon us, through Jesus Christ, our Saviour.

OUR Father which art in heaven, Hallowed be Thy name. Thy kingdom come. Thy will be done in earth, as it is in heaven. Give us this day our daily bread. And forgive us our debts, as we forgive our debtors. And lead us not into temptation, but deliver us from evil: For Thine is the kingdom, and the power, and the glory, for ever.—*Amen.*

Lord's Day Evening.

"I will say of the Lord, He is my refuge and my fortress: my God; in Him will I trust."

Let us Pray.

ALMIGHTY GOD, who dwellest on high, receiving the worship of the hosts of heaven, accept, we beseech Thee, the praises which, on earth, we offer unto Thee in the name of Jesus Christ our Lord. Let our prayer be set forth before Thee as incense, and the lifting up of our hands as the evening sacrifice.

We thank Thee, O God, for Thy works of creation and providence. All Thy works praise Thee, and Thy saints bless Thee. We thank Thee for that more perfect revelation of Thyself, which Thou hast given us in Thy Word. We bless Thee for those things which were written aforetime by holy men for our learning, that we, through patience and comfort of the Scriptures, might have hope. And, above all, we magnify Thy name, that Thou hast in these last days spoken unto us by Thy Son, whom Thou hast sent to be the Light of the world.

Cause Thy Holy Spirit so to shine into our hearts and minds, that we, being filled with the knowledge of Thy will, and animated with the hope of Thy promises, may in all things adorn the doctrine of our Lord and Saviour Jesus Christ.

Be pleased, O God, to follow with Thy blessing the instructions we have this day heard, and graciously receive the praises we have offered to Thee. Vouchsafe an answer to our prayers, and grant that all the services of our earthly Sabbaths may, by Thy grace, prepare us for the heavenly rest.

Hear us, O Father in heaven, as we pray for our brethren of mankind. Be pleased to make known the way of salvation to all who are yet in ignorance or error, and to hasten the time when the fulness of the Gentiles, together with the lost sheep of the house of Israel, shall be brought into the fold of the Good Shepherd. Be very gracious to Thy servants who have gone forth to preach among the heathen the unsearchable riches of Christ. Aid them in their labours; counsel them in their difficulties; defend them in their dangers; support them in their discouragements; and crown their efforts with abundant and increasing success.

Bless Thy whole Church; heal its divisions; reform its errors; cleanse it from its corruptions. Give grace to those who serve Thee in the ministry of the Word, that they may be faithful and zealous, watching for souls as those who must give an account. Deliver them from worldliness and selfishness, and make them earnest and active in Thy service in the world. Incline the hearts of parents to give heed to the godly training of their children; and grant that all children, nurtured in Thy fear, may steadfastly walk in the way of Thy commandments.

Father of mercies, extend Thy compassion to all in affliction. Give them support and comfort in their trials, and let Thy fatherly chastening fit them for the heavenly home.

And now, O God, we commit ourselves, and all our friends, to Thy care, beseeching Thee to defend us this night from all evil, and to bring us, if it please Thee, in safety to the light of a new day.

Graciously hear our prayers, which we offer in the name of Thy well-beloved Son, our Lord and Saviour.

OUR Father which art in heaven, Hallowed be Thy name. Thy kingdom come. Thy will be done in earth, as it is in heaven. Give us this day our daily bread. And forgive us our debts, as we forgive our debtors. And lead us not into temptation, but deliver us from evil: For Thine is the kingdom, and the power, and the glory, for ever.—*Amen.*

Monday Morning.

"Then shall we know, if we follow on to know the Lord: His going forth is prepared as the morning; and He shall come unto us as the rain, as the latter and former rain unto the earth."

LET US PRAY.

ALMIGHTY GOD, grant unto us the influences of the Holy Spirit, that we, who are called to the fellowship of Jesus Christ Thy Son, may in Him be led also into fellowship with Thee the Father.

We confess, O God, that our hearts have been estranged from Thee; that we have lived without Thee in the world; and that by our manifold sins we have provoked Thee to cast us away from Thy presence, and to withhold Thy tender mercies from us.

Have pity on us, for the sake of Thy beloved Son, in whom Thou art always well pleased. Put not away Thy servants in anger. Leave us not, neither forsake us, O God of our salvation. Draw nigh to us, and bring us nigh to Thee. And make us glad with the light of Thy countenance.

Give us grace, whereby we may be enabled in all our ways to acknowledge Thee. Help us to live near to Thee. Teach us to look to Thee as our very present help, and to cleave to Thee as our only satisfying portion. Be with us, O Father, everywhere, and at all times, in health or in sickness, in prosperity or in trouble, that Thy presence may sweeten and sanctify whatever befalls us. And cease not to guide and uphold us on our way, until Thou hast safely brought us to Thy heavenly kingdom, where we shall see Thee, and dwell with Thee for ever.

We give Thee thanks for the rest of the past night, and for the mercies of another morning. Let Thy presence go with us, and Thy grace help us, amidst all the duties and trials of the day. Enable us to prosecute the labours of the week in the spirit of those who have worshipped in Thy house, and who are guided by the words of heavenly truth. And whatsoever we are called to do, may we do it heartily, not with eye-service as men-pleasers, but with singleness of heart as unto Thee our God.

Extend, we pray Thee, the joy of Thy favour, and the comfort of Thy fellowship, to all our friends. Hide not Thy face from those who are in trouble. Speak peace to them that are afar off. Reclaim the erring. And bring men everywhere to know Thee, love Thee, and trust in Thee with all their heart. May Thy Holy Spirit enlighten, guide, and comfort all the children of men.

These, our humble supplications, we present to Thee

in the name of Jesus, Thy beloved Son, our Lord and Saviour.

OUR Father which art in heaven, Hallowed be Thy name. Thy kingdom come. Thy will be done in earth, as it is in heaven. Give us this day our daily bread. And forgive us our debts, as we forgive our debtors. And lead us not into temptation, but deliver us from evil: For thine is the kingdom, and the power, and the glory, for ever.—*Amen.*

Monday Evening.

"Commit thy works unto the Lord, and thy thoughts shall be established."

LET US PRAY.

O GOD, who knowest the secrets of every heart, and understandest our thoughts afar off; humble us under a sense of our unworthiness; and graciously pardon, for Christ's sake, our offences, which are naked and open in Thy sight.

Who, O God, can understand his errors? Cleanse Thou us from secret faults. Keep back Thy servants also from presumptuous sins, and let them not have dominion over us. Search us, O God, and know our hearts; try us, and know our thoughts; and see if there be any wicked way in us, and lead us in the way everlasting.

Show us what is wanting in us of the faith and love and obedience which Thou requirest.

Enable us, O God our strength, to watch and pray, lest we enter into temptation. Suffer us not to trust in our own strength, which is but weakness; or in our own wisdom, which is but folly; or in our own goodness, which is as a morning cloud or as the early dew, which goeth away. Keep us mindful that the heart is deceitful above all things, and desperately wicked; and that even when the spirit is willing, the flesh is weak. Teach us ever to look up to Thee for Thy promised aid, without which we can do nothing. And grant that, building ourselves up on our most holy faith, and praying in the Holy Ghost, we may keep ourselves in Thy love, looking for the mercy of our Lord Jesus Christ unto eternal life.

To Thy watchful providence, O God, we commit ourselves, and all who are dear to us, during the coming night. Grant us quiet sleep, and, if it please Thee, spare us to enjoy the blessings and discharge the duties of another day.

Father of mercies, we beseech Thee to have compassion on those who are tried with adversity and affliction. Provide for the destitute. Comfort the mourners. Lift up those who are bowed down with years. Relieve the sick. Spare useful lives. Support the dying, and prepare them for their change.

O God, who hast made of one blood all nations, and wouldst have all men to come to the knowledge of the truth, open, we pray Thee, a great and effectual door for the preaching of Thy blessed Gospel everywhere; and hasten the time when all the ends of the earth shall see its glorious light, and hear its joyful sound.

These, our prayers, we present for the sake of Jesus

Christ, Thy beloved Son, to whom, with Thee and with the Holy Spirit, be glory everlasting.

OUR Father which art in heaven, Hallowed be Thy name. Thy kingdom come. Thy will be done in earth, as it is in heaven. Give us this day our daily bread. And forgive us our debts, as we forgive our debtors. And lead us not into temptation, but deliver us from evil: For Thine is the kingdom, and the power, and the glory, for ever.—*Amen*.

Tuesday Morning.

"Cast away from you all your transgressions, whereby ye have transgressed; and make you a new heart and a new spirit: for why will ye die, O house of Israel?

"For I have no pleasure in the death of him that dieth, saith the Lord God: wherefore turn yourselves, and live ye."

Let us Pray.

ALMIGHTY GOD, on whom we ever depend, and without whom we can do nothing, we lift up our souls to Thee in prayer and supplication with thanksgiving. Thou art our God, early will we seek Thee.

We give Thee thanks for the rest of the past night, and now that the light of another day is shining on us, we humbly implore the continuance of Thy care, and yield ourselves up anew to Thy service.

Holy Father, we acknowledge that we are sinful creatures, who merit nothing at Thy hands. But putting our trust in the merits of Thy dear Son, in whom we have redemption through His blood, we pray Thee to forgive our sins, and to give us grace, that henceforth we may be able to glorify Thee.

O God, who desirest truth in the inward parts, and unto whom no services are acceptable but such as proceed from a pure and honest heart; fill our hearts, we pray Thee, with Thy love and Thy truth, and remove all evil motives from our minds. Save us from error, impenitence, and unbelief. Preserve us from insensibility of conscience. Deliver us from sinful tempers, from unholy thoughts and inordinate affections; from pride, envy, covetousness, and all uncharitableness. Inspire us with unfeigned love to Thee and to man. Enable us with all diligence to keep the heart, out of which are the issues of life.

Let Thy blessing rest on all who are under this roof. Give grace to all of us to discharge our several duties with uprightness, fidelity, and diligence. Bestow Thy favour on our relatives and friends. Have pity on those whom Thou hast visited with affliction, and give them the consolations of Thy grace. Look in mercy upon all mankind. May the light of the Gospel soon shine throughout all the world. Give the Holy Spirit to us, and to all who pray for the coming of Thy kingdom, that we may be constrained to work and to give, that the knowledge of the salvation of Jesus Christ may be made known to all mankind.

And now, O our God, we commit ourselves to Thee. Show us Thy ways; lead us in Thy truth, and teach us; for Thou art the God of our salvation; on Thee would we wait all the day. Graciously hear us, and grant an answer of peace, through Jesus Christ, our Lord.

OUR Father which art in heaven, Hallowed be Thy name. Thy kingdom come. Thy will be done in earth, as it is in heaven. Give us this day our daily bread. And forgive us our debts, as we forgive our debtors. And lead us not into temptation, but deliver us from evil: For Thine is the kingdom, and the power, and the glory, for ever.—*Amen.*

Tuesday Evening.

"It is better to trust in the Lord than to put confidence in man. It is better to trust in the Lord than to put confidence in princes."

LET US PRAY.

ALMIGHTY and most merciful God, in whom we live and move and have our being, impress us with a sense of our dependence on Thee, and enable us to trust in Thee with all our heart.

Lord, we believe; help Thou our unbelief. Lord, increase our faith, and grant that it may prevail over all fear and ignorance and doubt, to Thy glory and our exceeding comfort.

Give us full reliance on Thy grace, and in the

special care and kindness of Thy providence. Teach us to know Thee as our reconciled God in Jesus Christ, and strengthen and comfort us by the truth, that if Thou art for us, nothing can be against us, and that all things shall work together for good to them that love Thee.

Deliver us, we beseech Thee, from anxious thoughts and disquieting fears, and enable us to believe that Thou, our heavenly Father, who clothest the grass of the field and feedest the fowls of the air, wilt much more provide all things needful for us, Thy children. Whether it please Thee to give, or to withhold, or to take away from us any of this world's good things, make us entirely submissive to Thy will, trusting ever more in Thine eternal love as revealed to us in Jesus Christ our Lord.

Father of mercies, we thankfully acknowledge Thy care and kindness during the past day; and now, at the close of it, we commit ourselves to Thy keeping. We will lay ourselves down in peace and sleep, because Thou only makest us to dwell in safety.

Look with compassion, we beseech Thee, on all Thy people whom Thou hast afflicted. Help them to bow in meek submission to Thy will.

Extend Thy favour to all our brethren of mankind. Our heart's desire and prayer is, that they may be saved. Let the people praise Thee, O God; let all the people praise Thee.

Almighty God, who givest food to all flesh, regard our land, we beseech Thee, with Thy favour. Remember Thy promise that seed-time and harvest shall not cease while the earth remaineth, and send unto us favourable weather and fruitful seasons, that our fields may in due time yield an abundant increase, and our souls may rejoice in Thy bounty.

Sanctify us all by Thy Holy Spirit, and mercifully hear and answer these our prayers, which we offer in the name of Thine only-begotten Son, our Lord and Saviour.

OUR Father which art in heaven, Hallowed be Thy name. Thy kingdom come. Thy will be done in earth, as it is in heaven. Give us this day our daily bread. And forgive us our debts, as we forgive our debtors. And lead us not into temptation, but deliver us from evil: For Thine is the kingdom, and the power, and the glory, for ever.—*Amen.*

Wednesday Morning.

"Blessed are the meek: for they shall inherit the earth.

"Blessed are the peacemakers: for they shall be called the children of God."

LET US PRAY.

O LORD our God, who dwellest in the heavens, but humblest Thyself to behold the things that are in the earth; incline Thine ear to the voice of our supplications. Although we are unworthy of Thy favour by reason of our manifold offences, yet do we beseech Thee, in the name of Thy beloved Son, to receive us graciously; forgiving us those things for which our own hearts condemn us, and making us glad with the light of Thy countenance. Give us grace to show our sense of Thy mercy, not only by love to Thee who hast first loved us, but by kind and charitable dispositions towards all men, and by abounding in those peaceable fruits of righteousness, which are unto Thy praise and glory, through Christ Jesus our Lord.

O God, who art ever merciful and gracious, long-suffering and slow to anger; who hast not dealt with us after our sins, nor rewarded us according to our iniquities; give unto Thy servants a meek and quiet spirit, that we may not be easily provoked by wrongs, or quick to resent indignities; but that we may be patient toward all men, and ready to forgive, even as Thou, for Christ's sake, hast forgiven us.

Dispose us, in our intercourse with our fellow-men, to shun every occasion of discord. Help us to put away from us all bitterness, and wrath, and anger, and clamour, and evil speaking, with all malice. And teach us to love as brethren, to be pitiful, to be courteous, and to follow after the things which make for peace, and things whereby one may edify another.

Grant that peace may abide in this household, and that all the members of it may dwell together in unity. Bestow Thy favour on our relatives and friends. Reward with Thy bounty all who have done us good. Forgive all who have done or wished us evil, and enable us to forgive them from the heart.

Have pity on those who are in adversity. Enable them meekly to submit to Thy will; and sanctify Thy chastening for their good.

We pray for the peace and welfare of Thy Church. Grant that all divisions therein may cease; that its errors may be corrected; and that all its members may stand fast in one spirit, striving together with one mind for the faith of the Gospel.

We pray for the peace and prosperity of our native land; and for the enlightenment and conversion of all nations. Bless those who influence the thoughts and actions of men. Teach them, O God, to think and speak aright. Bless those who live by the labour of their hands. Teach them to be diligent and contented, and trusting in Thee. Remove all ignorance and superstition, all jealousy and discontent, from the people, and in Thy mercy cause strife and tumult everywhere to cease. And hasten the time, when the Prince of Peace shall take to Himself His great power, and reign over the whole earth; and when, under His dominion, nation shall no longer rise against nation, neither shall they learn war any more.

Graciously hear our petitions, which we offer to Thee in the name of Thy beloved Son, our Lord and Saviour.

OUR Father which art in heaven, Hallowed be Thy name. Thy kingdom come. Thy will be done in earth, as it is in heaven. Give us this day our daily bread. And forgive us our debts, as we forgive our debtors. And lead us not into temptation, but deliver us from evil: For Thine is the kingdom, and the power, and the glory, for ever.—*Amen.*

Wednesday Evening.

"Whosoever shall confess that Jesus is the Son of God, God dwelleth in him, and he in God. And we have known and believed the love that God hath to us. God is love; and he that dwelleth in love dwelleth in God, and God in him."

Let us Pray.

ALMIGHTY GOD, Father of mercies, who givest us richly all things to enjoy, we render praise to Thee for Thy great goodness. We bless Thee, that Thou hast created us by Thy power, and hast constantly upheld and preserved us by Thy providence. But above all, we magnify Thy name, that Thou hast so loved the world, as to give Thine only-begotten Son, that whosoever believeth in Him should not perish, but have everlasting life.

Fill our hearts with gratitude, we beseech Thee, for the great love wherewith Thou hast loved us. And enable us to show our sense of it, not with our lips only, but in our lives, by presenting our bodies a living sacrifice, holy and acceptable unto Thee.

Grant also, O God, that our souls may be inspired with warm and grateful affection towards Him who loved us and gave Himself for us. Reveal to us the excellences of His character, and cause us to see that He is altogether lovely. Teach us to adore the wonders of His grace, in that though He was rich, yet for our sakes He became poor, that we through His poverty might be made rich.

Strengthen us with might by Thy Spirit in the inner man, that Christ may dwell in our hearts by faith; and that we, being rooted and grounded in love, may be able to comprehend with all saints what is the breadth, and length, and depth, and height, and to know the love of Christ, which passeth knowledge.

Give us grace, that we may steadfastly cleave to Him, as one whom, not having seen, we love; and in whom, though now we see Him not, yet believing, we rejoice with joy unspeakable and full of glory. And grant that our love to Him may abound more and more, and that we may be led by it more and more zealously to do whatsoever He hath commanded us; until, having faithfully served Him on earth, we are taken to dwell with Him eternally in heaven.

O Thou Keeper of Israel, who never slumberest, watch over us this night, and keep us from all evil. Extend Thy favour and protection to our friends. Regard with tender pity those who are in affliction, and overrule the trials they are enduring for the everlasting welfare of their souls. Have mercy on those who are perishing for lack of knowledge; and hasten the time when all the ends of the earth shall be brought to the faith and obedience of Thy Gospel.

Grant these requests, O God, we beseech Thee, through Jesus Christ, our Lord.

OUR Father which art in heaven, Hallowed be Thy name. Thy kingdom come. Thy will be done in earth, as it is in heaven. Give us this day our

daily bread. And forgive us our debts, as we forgive our debtors. And lead us not into temptation, but deliver us from evil: For Thine is the kingdom, and the power, and the glory, for ever.—*Amen.*

Thursday Morning.

"I have longed for Thy salvation, O Lord; and Thy law is my delight. Let my soul live, and it shall praise Thee; and let Thy judgments help me."

Let us Pray.

O GOD, we come before Thee this morning with thanksgiving.

We thank Thee for Thine infinite wisdom, power, and goodness, and for Thy care of us in all the past.

We thank Thee for Thy wondrous love in redeeming the world from the guilt and punishment of sin by the blood of Thy dearly beloved Son, and from the power of sin by the grace of the Holy Spirit. We bless and praise Thee that Thou hast made us capable of knowing, loving, and serving Thee in righteousness and true holiness. And now, with the new morning light, we ask Thee for renewed power to do Thy will, and we would render unto Thee the glory which is Thy due.

Teach us to be just and righteous in our dealings with our fellow-men. Suffer us not to beguile any with deceitful words, or to injure any by evil deeds. Grant that integrity and uprightness may preserve us from seeking the advancement of our own interests, or the relief of our own necessities, by trespassing on the rights of others. Let it be our hearty desire to render unto all their dues, and our earnest endeavour to be faithful in that which is least, as well as in that which is greatest. And let our rejoicing be the testimony of our conscience, that in simplicity and godly sincerity, not with fleshly wisdom, but by the grace of God, we have our conversation in the world.

O God, who knowest how prone we are to abuse Thy bounty to our own hurt and Thy dishonour, give us grace that we may so use the good things which Thou hast provided for the sustenance of the body, that they may not in any wise be hurtful to the soul. Restrain us from intemperance of every kind. Help us to repress all inordinate desires for the riches, honours, and pleasures of this life. And may we ever remember that if we live after the flesh we shall die; but if, through the Spirit, we mortify the deeds of the body, we shall live.

Forgive our sins, and give us grace, that henceforth we may deny ourselves to all ungodliness and worldly lusts, and may lead a godly, righteous, and sober life, to the glory of Thy holy name.

Let Thy presence go with us this day to our appointed duties; and let Thy grace in all things be sufficient for us.

We commend to Thy favour our relatives and friends. Be Thou their God and guide in this world, in death their stay, and in the world to come their eternal portion. Reward with Thy bounty all who have done us good. Pardon and convert all who have done or wished us evil; and enable us to forgive them from the heart.

Bless and long preserve our Sovereign. Prosper all the interests of our country. Hasten the coming of Thy kingdom in the world.

God of all comfort, have pity on the afflicted. Assuage their griefs; relieve their sufferings; and overrule Thy chastening for their good. Have mercy on those who are drawing near to death. Let Thy grace sustain them.

Graciously hear and answer us, O God, according to Thy promises made to us in Christ Jesus, to whom, with Thee and with the Holy Spirit, be glory everlasting.

OUR Father which art in heaven, Hallowed be Thy name. Thy kingdom come. Thy will be done in earth, as it is in heaven. Give us this day our daily bread. And forgive us our debts, as we forgive our debtors. And lead us not into temptation, but deliver us from evil: For Thine is the kingdom, and the power, and the glory, for ever.—*Amen.*

Thursday Evening.

"The Lord is thy keeper: the Lord is thy shade upon thy right hand. The sun shall not smite thee by day, nor the moon by night."

LET US PRAY.

ALMIGHTY GOD, who by Thy wise providence hast ordered all our lot, and crowned us with unmerited loving-kindnesses, dispose us thankfully to acknowledge Thy goodness, and humbly to submit ourselves to Thy will.

Forgive, we beseech Thee, for Christ's sake, our lack of faith and hope. Forgive our impatience and discontent. Forgive us if we have failed to see Thy love in all Thy dealings with us; and by Thy grace enable us henceforth to rest contented in Thy holy will, and cheerfully to accept whatever Thou dost send.

Prepare us to receive evil as well as good at Thy hand, in the confident persuasion that Thou chastenest us, not for Thy pleasure, but for our profit, that we may be partakers of Thy holiness. Enable us to possess our souls in patience amidst the trials and troubles of our present condition, believing that our light affliction, which is but for a moment, worketh for us a far more exceeding and eternal weight of glory.

Teach us to count all things but loss for the excellency of the knowledge of Christ Jesus our Lord, in whom Thou hast blessed us with all spiritual and heavenly blessings. Satisfy our souls with His divine fulness, so that, whatever adversities befall us, we may be able cheerfully to submit to them.

Sanctify us by Thy Holy Spirit, and grant us that godliness with contentment, which is great gain.

And now, O God, we commit ourselves to Thee, who hast said that Thou wilt never leave us nor forsake us. Watch over us this night; deliver us from evil; and grant us quiet sleep under the shadow of Thy wings.

Regard with Thy favour our family and kindred, our friends and neighbours, and all who are connected with us. Do them good, and visit them with Thy salvation.

Bless the rich; and constrain them to use their abundance for Thy glory, and the good of men. Bless the poor; and give to them the heavenly riches, and a godly contentment with their lot. Bless all who labour with their hands, and grant to them health and strength, and perfect trust in Thee.

Help and pity the afflicted. And strengthen them with might, according to Thy glorious power, unto all patience and long-suffering with joyfulness.

Reveal Thy marvellous light to those who are in darkness, and increase everywhere the number of Thy people, who know Thy name, and put their trust in Thee.

Graciously hear our supplications, which we offer in the name of Thy beloved Son, our Lord and Saviour.

OUR Father which art in heaven, Hallowed be Thy name. Thy kingdom come. Thy will be done in earth, as it is in heaven. Give us this day our daily bread. And forgive us our debts, as we forgive our debtors. And lead us not into temptation, but deliver us from evil: For Thine is the kingdom, and the power, and the glory, for ever.—*Amen.*

Friday Morning.

"I will lift up mine eyes unto the hills, from whence cometh my help. My help cometh from the Lord, which made heaven and earth."

Let us Pray.

ALMIGHTY GOD, the Author of our being, the Preserver of our lives, the Redeemer of our souls, we acknowledge that we are Thine, and that all that we have is Thine. All our homage and obedience are due to Thee, and all that we know of Thee calls us to love and serve Thee, our Father and heavenly King.

Whom have we, O Lord, in heaven but Thee? And there is none upon earth that we desire beside Thee. O that there were such an heart in us, that we would fear Thee, and keep Thy commandments always, that it might be well with us and with our children for ever.

O our God, we are ashamed that hitherto our love to Thee has so little moved us, and that we have so greatly failed in Thy service. Pardon, we beseech Thee, our lack of zeal for the honour of Thy name. Enter not into judgment with us for the coldness of our affections, the fickleness of our purposes, and the weakness of our endeavours. And give us grace, that henceforth we may be able to yield Thee the full devotion of our hearts, and earnestly to employ all our faculties and talents in obedience to Thy will, and to Thy heavenly glory.

Almighty God, who workest in us both to will and to do of Thy good pleasure, strengthen us with might by Thy Spirit in the inner man, that we may be ready for every good word and work. Suffer us not to grow lukewarm in duty, nor to weary in welldoing. Fill our hearts with such love to Thee, that nothing may seem to us too hard to do, or too grievous to suffer for Thy sake. Above all, grant that our souls may be brought under the constraining power of redeeming love, so that we may live no longer unto ourselves, but unto Christ who loved us and gave Himself for us.

Giver of all good, we look up to Thee for the supply of our daily wants. Bestow upon us needful sustenance, and contentment therewith. Bless us in all the work of our hands, and aid us this day, we beseech Thee, in our several duties. Grant that we may be not slothful in business, but fervent in spirit, serving the Lord.

Bestow Thy favour and blessing on our friends. Give consolation to all who are in sorrow. Provide for the destitute. Deliver the oppressed. Support the aged. Relieve the sick. Prepare for their departure those who are about to die. Give Thy good Spirit in rich measure unto all, that by His aid they may be able to discern and keep Thy truth, and may be guided thereby through this life unto the heavenly kingdom.

Have pity on those who are perishing for lack of knowledge. Give to Thy Son the heathen for His inheritance, and the uttermost parts of the earth for His possession; and stir our hearts, and the hearts of all Thy people, to greater zeal, liberality, and prayer, in seeking the diffusion of Thy Gospel throughout the world.

Graciously hear us, for the sake of Jesus Christ, our Lord and Saviour.

OUR Father which art in heaven, Hallowed be Thy name. Thy kingdom come. Thy will be done in earth, as it is in heaven. Give us this day our

daily bread. And forgive us our debts, as we forgive our debtors. And lead us not into temptation, but deliver us from evil: For Thine is the kingdom, and the power, and the glory, for ever.—*Amen.*

Friday Evening.

"What is man, that Thou shouldest magnify him? and that Thou shouldest set Thine heart upon him? and that Thou shouldest visit him every morning, and try him every moment?"

Let us Pray.

ALMIGHTY and everlasting God, who resistest the proud, and givest grace to the humble; grant, we beseech Thee, that we may not exalt ourselves, and provoke Thine indignation, but may bow down and receive the gifts of Thy mercy, through Jesus Christ our Lord.

We thank Thee that Thou, who inhabitest eternity and whose name is Holy, hast promised to dwell with him also that is of a contrite and humble spirit, to revive the spirit of the humble, and the heart of the contrite ones.

We acknowledge with shame that we have often sinned against Thee, by cherishing proud and vain imaginations, by thinking of ourselves more highly than we ought to think, and by claiming pre-eminence above our brethren.

Pardon, we beseech Thee, wherein we have thus offended Thee. And give us grace, that henceforth we may be enabled faithfully to render that which Thou requirest of us, by doing justly, loving mercy, and walking humbly with Thee our God.

Give us the grace of humility, and grant that by the teaching of the Holy Spirit we may learn that we of ourselves have nothing, and can do nothing, and that Thou art the Giver of all.

Give us also, we beseech Thee, O God, the grace of charity, which vaunteth not itself, is not puffed up, and doth not behave itself unseemly; so that, in all our intercourse with our fellow-men, we may do nothing through strife or vainglory, but that each of us may in lowliness of mind esteem others better than himself.

Help us to imitate the pattern of humility which our blessed Lord and Saviour hath set before us, that learning of Him who was meek and lowly in heart, we may find rest unto our souls, and hereafter be partakers of His glory in His heavenly kingdom.

Bestow the like blessings, we pray Thee, on our friends. Let the mind that was in Christ Jesus be found in all His people. Specially grant unto Thine afflicted servants a spirit of humble submission to Thy will. And so further the cause of pure religion throughout the world, that men everywhere may serve Thee with humility. Let not the wise man glory in his wisdom, nor the mighty man in his might, nor the rich man in his riches; but he that glorieth, let him glory in the Lord.

Father of mercies, we thankfully acknowledge Thy goodness to us throughout the past day; and we humbly commit ourselves, and all whom we love, to Thy watchful care during this night. Suffer no evil to befall us, nor any plague to come nigh our dwelling. Grant us quiet sleep, and raise us on the morrow with renewed strength for the duties which may then await us.

Hear our humble supplications, we beseech Thee, and do for us abundantly, above all that we ask or think, through Jesus Christ, our Saviour.

OUR Father which art in heaven, Hallowed be Thy name. Thy kingdom come. Thy will be done in earth, as it is in heaven. Give us this day our daily bread. And forgive us our debts, as we forgive our debtors. And lead us not into temptation, but deliver us from evil: For Thine is the kingdom, and the power, and the glory, for ever.—*Amen.*

Saturday Morning.

"Blessed is the people that know the joyful sound: they shall walk, O Lord, in the light of Thy countenance."

Let us Pray.

O GOD, we worship and bow down; we kneel before Thee, our Lord and Maker; for Thou art our God; and we are the people of Thy pasture, and the sheep of Thy hand. We praise Thee for all Thy goodness, and for the special mercies we have received from Thee in Christ Jesus our Saviour.

Pardon, we beseech Thee, our ungrateful returns for Thy loving-kindnesses. Deal not with us according to our sins, but pardon us, and give us grace, that henceforth we may be able to show our sense of Thy goodness by a life of cheerful obedience to Thy will.

Almighty God, who didst in the beginning command the light to shine out of darkness, and hast again made the light of the sun to arise upon the world in the morning of another day; let it please Thee so to illuminate our souls with the grace of Thy Holy Spirit, that we may be guided in the paths of righteousness, and brought to know Thee and Thy Son Jesus Christ, whom to know is life eternal.

Deliver us, we pray Thee, from ignorance and delusion, from prejudice and passion, from pride and self-confidence, and from every evil influence that opposes the entrance of Thy truth into our minds.

Give to us humble, teachable, and obedient hearts, that we may meekly receive whatsoever Thou hast taught us.

Make us ready to believe, where we cannot see; and willing to trust, where we cannot comprehend.

Endue us with a right judgment in all things, that we may know the things that are true, and approve the things that are excellent. And grant that Thy truth may so richly dwell in us, in all wisdom and spiritual understanding, that by it we may be built up in holiness and comfort through faith unto salvation.

Graciously hear us, O God, while we plead with Thee for our fellow-men. Send forth the light of Thy Gospel throughout the world, to enlighten and reclaim the nations that are in darkness. Take away from the hearts of Thine ancient people the veil that hinders them from seeing the fulfilment of Thy promises made unto their fathers. Arrest the progress of infidelity and ungodliness. Hasten the downfall of idolatry and superstition. Stand by Thy missionary servants, giving them grace to be faithful, and the comforting assurance of Thy presence and blessing. Pour out Thy Holy Spirit upon all flesh, that all men may know Thee, from the least unto the greatest.

We pray for the peace and welfare of Thy whole Church. Cleanse it from impurity. Preserve it from error. Enlighten and guide all pastors and teachers, that they may fully know and faithfully proclaim Thy Gospel. And grant that Thy people everywhere, being instructed by words of faith, may in all things adorn the doctrine of our Lord and Saviour Jesus Christ.

Father of mercies and God of all comfort, look down in pity on the poor, the sorrowful, the sick, and the dying. Succour and relieve them according to their need, and grant that their present affliction may work for them a far more exceeding and eternal weight of glory.

Graciously hear and answer us, O Lord, according to the fulness of Thy mercy in Christ Jesus; to whom, with Thee and with the Holy Spirit, be glory everlasting.

OUR Father which art in heaven, Hallowed be Thy name. Thy kingdom come. Thy will be done in earth, as it is in heaven. Give us this day our daily bread. And forgive us our debts, as we forgive our debtors. And lead us not into temptation, but deliver us from evil: For Thine is the kingdom, and the power, and the glory, for ever.—*Amen.*

Saturday Evening.

"Thy statutes have been my songs in the house of my pilgrimage. I have remembered Thy name, O Lord, in the night, and have kept Thy law. This I had, because I kept Thy precepts."

Let us Pray.

ALMIGHTY and everlasting God, by whose good hand upon us we have been brought to the close of another week; we give Thee thanks for the patience and forbearance which, in the time that is past, Thou hast manifested toward us, and for all the blessings which we have received at Thy hand. It is of Thy mercies, O Lord, that we are not consumed; because Thy compassions fail not. We have daily provoked Thee to anger with our sins, and yet Thou hast daily loaded us with benefits. We have often abused the riches of Thy long-suffering, and slighted the things which belong unto our peace; and yet Thou hast mercifully lengthened our day of grace, and multiplied our opportunities of repentance.

Lord God, merciful and gracious, who desirest not the death of a sinner, but rather that he turn from his wickedness and live, incline us with all our hearts to turn unto Thee, and cause Thy face to shine upon us, that we may be saved. Bestow upon us, through the merits of Jesus Christ, the forgiveness of our past sins. And enable us, by the grace of Thy Holy Spirit, to amend our lives according to Thy Word, and to bring forth abundantly those fruits of holy obedience which are, through Jesus Christ, unto the praise and glory of Thy name.

O God, who hast taught us in Thy Word that it is appointed unto all men once to die, and after death the judgment, impress us with a sense of our frailty, and so teach us to number our days, that we may apply our hearts unto wisdom.

O Christ, our life, dwell Thou in us, that, by Thy power, we may escape from sin and death, and may have part in the life everlasting.

O Holy Spirit, keep us in safety continually, that our whole spirit, and soul, and body may be preserved blameless unto the coming of our Lord Jesus Christ.

Heavenly Father, we acknowledge Thy past goodness, and humbly beseech Thee to bless us still. Watch over us this night. Grant us refreshing sleep. Mercifully spare us to see the light of Thy holy day, and grant that we may awake with hearts duly prepared to enjoy its privileges and to discharge its duties.

Graciously hear us, O God, while we plead for all our fellow-men. Provide for the poor. Instruct the ignorant. Reclaim the erring. Comfort the afflicted. Be the guide of the young, and the strength of the aged; the orphan's stay, and the stranger's shield. Deliver those who are in danger or distress. Prepare for their great change those who are about to die.

Look in mercy on the whole human race. Enlighten and convert the nations that are yet in darkness. Watch over Thy flock wherever they be scattered. Gather both Jews and Gentiles into Thy fold. And hasten the time when there shall be one fold and one Shepherd.

Hear us, O God, and graciously accept us, through Jesus Christ, Thy well-beloved Son, to whom, with Thee and with the Holy Spirit, be all honour and glory, world without end.

OUR Father which art in heaven, Hallowed be Thy name. Thy kingdom come. Thy will be done in earth, as it is in heaven. Give us this day our daily bread. And forgive us our debts, as we forgive our debtors. And lead us not into temptation, but deliver us from evil: For Thine is the kingdom, and the power, and the glory, for ever.—*Amen.*

Prayers for Sacramental Occasions.

Morning Prayer in Preparation for the Holy Communion.

"Come now, and let us reason together, saith the Lord: Though your sins be as scarlet, they shall be as white as snow; though they be red like crimson, they shall be as wool."

"Him that cometh unto me I will in no wise cast out."

LET US PRAY.

LORD GOD, merciful and gracious, who art of purer eyes than to behold iniquity, but hast promised to receive into Thy favour, for Christ's sake, such as are truly penitent, we humble ourselves before Thee under a deep sense of our unworthiness, and ask at this time the aid of Thy Holy Spirit, that we may approach Thee with sorrow for our sins, and an earnest desire after true holiness.

We have broken Thy holy laws. We have been unthankful for Thy benefits. We have slighted the calls of Thy Word, and the chastenings and warnings of Thy providence. We have loved the creature more than the Creator, and have preferred our own ease and pleasure to Thy glory.

We have sinned against our brethren of mankind, by pride and envy, by malice and uncharitableness;

and we have harboured evil thoughts, cherished impure affections, suffered our hearts to be overcharged with the cares, and vanities, and pleasures of this life, and neglected the things which belong unto our peace.

O most merciful God, who of Thy great love hast given Thine only-begotten Son to be the propitiation for our sins, and hast declared Thine acceptance of His sacrifice, in that Thou hast raised Him from the dead, increase, we beseech Thee, our faith in Him; and grant that Thy Holy Spirit, while convincing us of sin, may enable us to take unto our hearts the blessed assurance of Thy forgiveness and fatherly kindness, through Jesus Christ our Lord; so that we may be filled with all peace and joy in believing, and may abound in hope through the power of the Holy Ghost.

Give us grace, also, whereby we may be enabled to bring forth fruits meet for repentance. Grant that, with godly sorrow for the past, and with sincere purpose of obedience for the future, we may turn our feet unto Thy testimonies, and make haste to keep Thy commandments.

We give Thee thanks for the prospect Thou art affording us of showing forth the death of our Redeemer, and partaking of the symbols of His broken body and shed blood. Aid us in all our preparatory exercises of prayer, and self-examination, and repentance. Search us, O God, and know our hearts; try us, and know our thoughts; and see if there be any wicked way in us, and lead us in the way everlasting.

Meet with us, we beseech Thee, in Thy courts, and help us to worship Thee in spirit and in truth. Enable Thy ministering servants to speak to us a word in season; and grant that their preaching may be accompanied with the demonstration and power of Thy Holy Spirit.

Let Thy Word everywhere have free course and be glorified, and hasten the time when it shall be preached throughout the whole world.

We commend our friends to Thy friendship; our benefactors to Thy bounty; our enemies to Thy forgiveness; and all the children of adversity to Thy tender compassion.

Graciously hear us, O God, and have mercy upon us, for the sake of Thy beloved Son, who hath taught us to pray, saying—

OUR Father which art in heaven, Hallowed be Thy name. Thy kingdom come. Thy will be done in earth, as it is in heaven. Give us this day our daily bread. And forgive us our debts, as we forgive our debtors. And lead us not into temptation, but deliver us from evil: For Thine is the kingdom, and the power, and the glory, for ever.—*Amen.*

Evening Prayer in Preparation for the Holy Communion.

Let us search and try our ways, and turn again unto the Lord."

"Turn Thou us unto Thee, O Lord, and we shall be turned; renew our days as of old."

Let us Pray.

O GOD, who inhabitest eternity, whose name is Holy, look down in the greatness of Thy compassion on us Thine unworthy children assembled before Thee. Graciously hear the confessions and prayers which we have this day made to Thee in the name of Thy beloved Son. Give us the spirit of true repentance, and have pity upon us, and forgive us, for unto Thee, O Lord our God, belong mercies and forgivenesses, though we have rebelled against Thee.

Comfort our hearts, we beseech Thee, with a full persuasion of Thy fatherly mercy in Jesus Christ our Saviour; and let a sense of Thine undeserved goodness excite in us a holy dread of offending Thee, and an earnest desire in all things to obey Thee. And being redeemed with the precious blood of Christ, may we no longer live as if we were our own, but yield up ourselves entirely to Thy service, and glorify Thee in our bodies and in our spirits, which are Thine.

We thank Thee for the prospect we now have of joining in that holy ordinance in which our Redeemer's sufferings are commemorated, and the precious blessings purchased by His death are represented and sealed to His faithful people. We acknowledge our unworthiness of so great a privilege. We confess that we have not used, as we ought, the blessed privileges of past communions to Thy glory and for our own spiritual good. We deeply lament that our holy impressions at the table of the Lord have so often been effaced, and that our solemn vows have so often been forgotten. O Lord, lay not these sins to our charge. And now that Thou art once more inviting us to sit down at the table of the Lord, enable us to go thither with more simplicity and godly sincerity than hitherto; with a livelier faith, a warmer love, a deeper penitence; with hearts more humbly dependent on Thy grace, and more firmly devoted to Thy service.

To this end may it please Thee to bless unto us the holy services in which we have this day been engaged, and the instructions which have been addressed to us from the Scriptures. Let not Thy word return unto Thee void. May its precious truths abide in our minds, and its holy fruits be manifest in our conduct.

And now, O God, we cast ourselves on Thy care. Watch over us during the darkness of the coming night. Grant us quiet sleep, and, if it please Thee, preserve us to see the light of another day.

Bestow Thy favour on our friends and fellow-worshippers. Cause them to see the good of Thy chosen, and visit them with Thy salvation.

Bless all ranks and conditions of men among us. Enable them faithfully to serve and honour Thee in whatsoever calling or station Thou hast allotted to them.

Impart all needful consolation and support to the poor, the sick, the sorrowful, and the dying. Instruct the ignorant; arouse the careless; strengthen the weak; confirm the wavering. Diffuse the glorious light of Thy Gospel among those who are sitting in darkness and in the shadow of death; and hasten the time when all the kingdoms of the world shall become the kingdoms of the Lord and of His Christ.

Graciously hear our humble supplications, and do to us abundantly above all that we ask or think, through Jesus Christ our Lord.

OUR Father which art in heaven, Hallowed be Thy name. Thy kingdom come. Thy will be done in earth, as it is in heaven. Give us this day our daily bread. And forgive us our debts, as we forgive our debtors. And lead us not into temptation, but deliver us from evil: For Thine is the kingdom, and the power, and the glory, for ever.—*Amen.*

Morning of a Communion Sunday.

"Sing unto the Lord, bless His name; show forth His salvation from day to day.

"Enter into His gates with thanksgiving, and into His courts with praise: be thankful unto Him, and bless His name."

LET US PRAY.

ALMIGHTY GOD, Father of our Lord Jesus Christ, who hast given us through Him free access to Thy presence, and art graciously inviting us, on this Thy holy day, to the worship of Thy house and the fellowship of Thy table, bestow upon us the grace of Thy Holy Spirit, that we may serve Thee acceptably with reverence and godly fear.

Impress our minds, we beseech Thee, with a just sense of the adorable attributes of Thy character. Fill our hearts with lively gratitude for the countless and unceasing bounties of Thy Providence. Above all, let our souls be stirred up to bless Thee for the riches of Thy grace, and to give unto Thee the glory that is due for Thine inestimable love in our redemption.

We magnify and praise Thy holy name for having so loved the world as to give Thine only-begotten Son, that whosoever believeth in Him should not perish, but have everlasting life. We thank Thee that He was made flesh and dwelt among us; that He fulfilled all righteousness and went about doing good; that He humbled Himself and became obedient unto death, being wounded for our transgressions and bruised for our iniquities. We thank Thee that He rose from the dead, ascended into heaven, and being by the right hand of God exalted, received for us of the Father the promise of the Holy Spirit. We thank Thee that, having gone to prepare a place for His people, He will come again to receive them unto Himself, that where He is, there they may be also.

What shall we render unto Thee, O Lord, for all Thy benefits toward us? We will take the cup of salvation, and call upon Thy name, and pay our vows to Thee in the presence of Thy people. Thou hast delivered our souls from death, our eyes from tears, and our feet from falling. Help us to walk before Thee in the land of the living, seeking our rest in

Thee, and presenting our bodies a living sacrifice, holy and acceptable unto God, which is our reasonable service.

Blessed be Thy name, O God of our salvation, for the renewed opportunity Thou art giving us of observing the holy sacrament of the Supper. Prepare us, we beseech Thee, for this ordinance, according to the preparation of the sanctuary. Confirm our faith in those great mysteries of redeeming grace which we are this day to show forth. Inspire us with ardent love to the Saviour. Work in us unfeigned sorrow for our sins. Give us sincere and humble purposes of new obedience, that we may with a true heart devote ourselves to His service. And enable us, while partaking of this ordinance, to feed by faith on the blessings represented by it, to our spiritual nourishment and growth in grace.

Bestow Thy favour on all our fellow-worshippers, and grant that they may be united to us in the bonds of charity, as becometh those who are brethren in the Lord. Be very gracious to Thy ministering servants, and give them richly to enjoy in their own souls the comforts and blessings they are honoured to dispense to others. Supply the lack of ordinances to those who are withheld by infirmity or affliction from worshipping in Thy house, and communicating at Thy table. Visit them also with the comforts of Thy fellowship, and satisfy their souls with Thy goodness. Bless Thy Church Universal. Let grace, mercy, and peace be multiplied unto all that love the Lord Jesus in sincerity.

And now, O God, our hope is in Thee. If Thy presence go not with us, carry us not up hence. Be with us in all the duties that await us. Make Thy grace sufficient for us. And grant that all the words of our mouth, and all the meditations of our heart, may be acceptable in Thy sight, through Jesus Christ, our Lord and only Saviour.

OUR Father which art in heaven, Hallowed be Thy name. Thy kingdom come. Thy will be done in earth, as it is in heaven. Give us this day our daily bread. And forgive us our debts, as we forgive our debtors. And lead us not into temptation, but deliver us from evil: For Thine is the kingdom, and the power, and the glory, for ever.—*Amen*.

Evening of a Communion Sunday.

"But to us there is but one God, the Father, of whom are all things, and we in Him; and one Lord Jesus Christ, by whom are all things, and we by Him."

"I will sacrifice unto Thee with the voice of thanksgiving; I will pay that that I have vowed. Salvation is of the Lord."

Let us Pray.

ALMIGHTY GOD, Father of mercies, from whom cometh down every good and perfect gift, we bless and praise Thy name for all Thy benefits. We thank Thee that Thou hast provided for us all things needful to sustain us in the present life, and that Thou hast also been pleased to feed us with that spiritual food whereby our souls may be nourished unto life eternal.

Fill our hearts with gratitude, we beseech Thee, for what we have this day seen, and heard, and tasted, and handled of the Word of Life; for Jesus Christ, who hath been evidently set forth crucified among us; and for the memorials and pledges of His dying love, of which we have been privileged to partake. May every good impression made upon us by the solemnities of a communion season be deepened and confirmed. May the vows and resolutions we have formed at the table of the Lord be remembered and fulfilled. May the spiritual nourishment and comfort we have there received strengthen us for the duties and trials which await us, so that we may be enabled to go on our way with gladness.

Help us, O God, in all things to walk worthy of the good confession we have witnessed before many brethren. Suffer us not to return to those sins which we have solemnly renounced as the hateful and accursed things that crucified the Lord of glory. Let us not be neglectful of those duties which we have promised to render to Him, as His ransomed and peculiar people. Enable us always to bear about with us in the body the dying of the Lord Jesus, that the life also of Jesus may be made manifest in our mortal flesh. And may the love of Christ constrain us to live no longer unto ourselves, but unto Him who died for us and rose again.

Gracious Lord, without whom we can do nothing, but through whom we can do all things, restrain us from self-confidence and presumption, and teach us humbly to trust in Thee. Hold Thou up our goings in Thy paths, that our footsteps slip not. Enable us to be steadfast and unmovable, always abounding in the work of the Lord; that when our course in this life is ended, we may be admitted to the supper of the Lamb, and may drink wine new with Him in the kingdom of His Father.

We commend to Thy favour our friends and fellow-worshippers, and more especially those who, on this occasion, have joined with us in commemorating the Saviour's death. May their hearts be comforted, being knit together in love. And as they have received Christ Jesus the Lord, so may they walk in Him, rooted and built up in Him, stablished in the faith, and abounding therein with thanksgiving. Be gracious to the young; confirm them in the truth, and keep them from all the evil that is in the world. Support the aged under the burden of their infirmities, and cheer them with the hope that Thou wilt never leave them nor forsake them.

Abundantly bless Thy ministering servants who have dispensed to us the word and bread of life.

Bestow Thy blessing on Thy whole Church. And hasten the time when the fulness of the Gentiles and the dispersed of Israel shall be gathered into Thy fold.

To Thy fatherly care, O God, we commend ourselves, and all who are near and dear to us, this night; beseeching Thee to defend us from all evil, and to bring us in safety to the light of another day.

And now, O God of peace, who broughtest again from the dead our Lord Jesus, that great Shepherd of the sheep, through the blood of the everlasting covenant; make us perfect in every good work to do Thy will, working in us that which is well-pleasing in Thy sight, through Jesus Christ; to whom be glory for ever and ever.

OUR Father which art in heaven, Hallowed be Thy name. Thy kingdom come. Thy will be done in earth, as it is in heaven. Give us this day our daily bread. And forgive us our debts, as we forgive our debtors. And lead us not into temptation, but deliver us from evil: For Thine is the kingdom, and the power, and the glory, for ever.—*Amen.*

Service for the Sick,

With Special Prayers for use in the Sick-room.

"Call upon me in the day of trouble: I will deliver thee, and thou shalt glorify me."

"In the day of my trouble I will call upon Thee: for Thou wilt answer me."

LET US PRAY.

O GOD, who ever governest Thy creatures with tender affection, incline Thine ear to our supplication; graciously regard this Thy servant who is suffering from bodily sickness, visit *him* with Thy salvation, and bestow the medicine of heavenly grace, through Jesus Christ our Lord.

O Almighty God, who by the might of Thy command drivest away from men's bodies all sickness and infirmity, be present in Thy goodness to this Thy servant, that *his* weakness may be banished and *his* strength recalled; and *his* health being thereupon restored, *he* may bless Thy holy name. Grant unto *him* the spirit of true repentance; and to *him*, being penitent, be Thou pleased, for Christ's sake, to grant remission of all sins, and grace unto holiness, the end of which is eternal life, through Jesus Christ our Lord.

Give, we beseech of Thee, O Lord, unto *him* an abiding and sure faith in Thee, so that all fear being removed, *he* may possess *his* soul in peace, and may bear with patience whatever further trial Thou dost send.

Give a bright and cheering hope that *his* spirit fail not in times of pain or weariness; but that *he* may be comforted by a sense of the heavenly sympathy of Jesus Christ, who bore the most bitter agony of the cross to save mankind.

Give unto Thy servant above all things, we pray Thee, power to rest in Thy fatherly love, as revealed in Jesus Christ the great Physician, that *he* may not fear any issue of this sickness, even though it be unto death.

Give Thy Holy Spirit in such measure that in this time of affliction *his* soul may be purified by trial and lifted up to the heavenly things which accompany salvation. Grant unto *him* the comforts of Thy Word, assurance of Thy favour, and a firm belief that all Thy good promises are true in Jesus Christ Thy Son our Saviour.

Prepare us all, O God, for whatever trials or sorrows may await us. And grant that, whether in health or in sickness, in joy or in grief, in life or in death, we may be enabled to glorify Thy name, and may be made meet for inheriting Thy heavenly kingdom, through Jesus Christ our Lord.—*Amen.*

Read.

Psalm cxxi.

I WILL lift up mine eyes unto the hills, from whence cometh my help.

My help cometh from the Lord, which made heaven and earth.

He will not suffer thy foot to be moved: He that keepeth thee will not slumber.

Behold, He that keepeth Israel shall neither slumber nor sleep.

The Lord is thy keeper; the Lord is thy shade upon thy right hand.

The sun shall not smite thee by day, nor the moon by night.

The Lord shall preserve thee from all evil: He shall preserve thy soul.

The Lord shall preserve thy going out, and thy coming in, from this time forth, and even for evermore.

Isaiah xliii. 1-3.

BUT now thus saith the Lord that created thee, O Jacob, and He that formed thee, O Israel, Fear not: for I have redeemed thee, I have called thee by thy name; thou art mine.

When thou passest through the waters, I will be with thee; and through the rivers, they shall not overflow thee: when thou walkest through the fire, thou shalt not be burned; neither shall the flame kindle upon thee.

For I am the Lord thy God, the Holy One of Israel, thy Saviour.

1 *Peter* i. 3-9.

BLESSED be the God and Father of our Lord Jesus Christ, which according to His abundant mercy hath begotten us again unto a lively hope, by the resurrection of Jesus Christ from the dead,

To an inheritance incorruptible, and undefiled, and that fadeth not away, reserved in heaven for you,

Who are kept by the power of God through faith unto salvation ready to be revealed in the last time:

Wherein ye greatly rejoice, though now for a season if need be, ye are in heaviness through manifold temptations;

That the trial of your faith, being much more precious than of gold that perisheth, though it be tried with fire, might be found unto praise and honour and glory at the appearing of Jesus Christ:

Whom having not seen, ye love; in whom, though now ye see Him not, yet believing, ye rejoice with joy unspeakable and full of glory:

Receiving the end of your faith, even the salvation of your souls.

LET US PRAY.

WE pray Thee, O Father in heaven, to bless to Thy servant these Thine own words of promise and of heavenly comfort. May *he* hope in Thy word. Be Thou *his* hiding-place and shield. Comfort *him*, O God, and quicken *him* after Thy loving-kindness;

for Thou art a present help in every time of trouble. Strengthen *him* in the day-time when suffering and faint. Cause the light of Thy presence to cheer *him* in the night-watches, when the spirit is filled with fear; and grant that, *his* faith being rooted and grounded in Thee, in *him* patience may have her perfect work.

In place of the intercessions which follow, the Special Prayer which has reference to the case of the sick person may be used, concluding with the Lord's Prayer and Blessing.

MERCIFUL FATHER, who hast taught us in Thy Holy Word that Thou dost not willingly afflict the children of men, look with compassion, we beseech Thee, on this Thy servant.

Sanctify to *him* Thy fatherly correction, that it may yield in *him* the peaceable fruits of righteousness. Teach *him* to submit with meekness to Thy will. Comfort *him* with a persuasion of Thy favour. Support *him* with the hope of eternal life.

We earnestly pray that, if it seem good to Thee, Thou wouldst bless the means employed for *his* recovery, that *his* sufferings may be relieved, *his* health restored, and *his* days prolonged to serve Thee on the earth. But if Thou hast appointed that this sickness shall be unto death, prepare *him*, O God, to depart in peace, and mercifully receive *him* into those blessed mansions which Thou art reserving in heaven for the faithful.

Give to *him*, O Father in heaven, assurance of Thy favour. Give to *him*, O Christ, the peace which the world cannot give. Give to *him*, O Holy Spirit, the light and comfort which can guide through life and through death.

OUR Father which art in heaven, Hallowed be Thy name. Thy kingdom come. Thy will be done in earth, as it is in heaven. Give us this day our daily bread. And forgive us our debts, as we forgive our debtors. And lead us not into temptation, but deliver us from evil: For Thine is the kingdom, and the power, and the glory, for ever.—*Amen.*

Blessing.

THE grace of our Lord Jesus Christ, and the love of God, and the communion of the Holy Ghost, be with us all.—*Amen.*

Special Prayers for the Sick, which may either be introduced where marked in the "Service for the Sick," or used alone.

I.

FOR A SICK CHILD.

ALMIGHTY and most merciful Father, to whom alone belong the issues of life and death; look down, we beseech Thee, in the greatness of Thy compassion, on this suffering child. O God, who dost not afflict willingly the children of men, have mercy upon *him*. Bless the means used for *his* recovery, and, if it please Thee, remove *his* sickness, and prolong *his* days on earth. Above all, grant that *his* soul may be sanctified by the grace of Thy Holy Spirit, and saved through the mediation of Thy beloved Son, who hath taught us to bring little children unto Him, and hath graciously assured us, that of such is the kingdom of heaven.

If it be Thy will to spare *him* in the land of the living, grant that *he* may be enabled by Thy grace faithfully to serve Thee in *his* day and generation. But if it seem to Thee good to remove *him* from us, we pray that Thou wouldst receive *him* into Thy heavenly kingdom.

Comfort the hearts of *his* sorrowing friends. Enable them to cast their care on Thee, who carest for them. Teach them to submit with meekness to

Thy will. And overrule Thy fatherly discipline for their spiritual good, through Jesus Christ our Lord. —*Amen.*

II.

PRAYER FOR ONE WHOSE SICKNESS HAS BEEN LONG CONTINUED.

O GOD, Creator and Preserver of all things, look with compassion, we beseech Thee, on Thy servant, whom Thou hast seen meet to visit with long-continued sickness.

Have mercy on *him*, for *he* is desolate and afflicted. Receive *him* into Thy fatherly protection; for *he* hath recourse in *his* adversity to Thee alone. Though *he* be sore troubled, Thou canst send deliverance; though cast down, Thou canst lift *him* up; though weak and trembling, Thou canst give *him* strength and courage; though conscious of great and manifold transgressions, Thou canst make *him* holy.

Vouchsafe, O God, to *him* Thy mercy for the sake of Thy beloved Son.

We pray Thee to arrest *his* malady and to restore *his* health. But if it seem to Thee good to protract *his* trials, give *him* strength to bear them. Teach *him* to regard *his* present distresses as the wise and merciful corrections of *his* Father in heaven. Let Thy Holy Spirit settle in *his* heart those precious promises which are made to us in Christ Jesus, so that *he* may patiently wait all the days of *his* appointed time, until *his* change come; and when the hour of *his* departure is at hand, support *him* with the hopes and consolations of Thy Gospel, that, trusting in Thy Word, *his* soul may depart in peace.

May it also please Thee, most merciful Father, to strengthen and comfort *his* relatives and friends, and all who minister to *him* in *his* affliction, that they faint not through overmuch labour and anxiety. Help them to cast their burden upon Thee, with the comfortable persuasion that Thou wilt sustain them. And let Thy chastening, though for the present grievous, yield in them afterwards the peaceable fruits of righteousness. These things we ask, O God, trusting in the mercy of Jesus Christ our Lord.—*Amen.*

III.

FOR ONE ABOUT TO UNDERGO A SERIOUS SURGICAL OPERATION.

O GOD, we commend to Thee, through Jesus Christ our Lord, this Thy servant in an hour of pain and fearfulness. Give *him* strength to bear with fortitude what lies before *him*. May *his* faith in Thee, and in Christ *his* Saviour, strengthen *him* and cheer *him*. May *he* as *he* suffers, remember what Christ has for *him* suffered. Grant wisdom, courage, and tenderness to *his* physicians; and, if it be Thy will, may what they do work in *him* a lasting cure. May *he* so patiently bear the wounding of *his* mortal body, that the discipline may tend to *his* growth in grace, and may *he*, by Thy mercy, be spared yet many days in the land of the living and place of hope, to thank and glorify Thee, who art a very present help in trouble. Grant this, we beseech Thee, O God, for Christ's sake.—*Amen.*

IV.

IN CASE OF SUDDEN ILLNESS OR ACCIDENT.

ALMIGHTY GOD, who smitest and healest, who killest and makest alive, while none can stay Thy hand; give ear, we beseech Thee, to our earnest supplications in behalf of this, Thy servant, whom Thou hast visited with sudden and severe affliction. Be pleased, O Lord, to deliver *him*; O Lord, make haste to help *him*. Quicken *him* for Thy name's sake; and for Thy righteousness' sake bring *his* soul out of trouble. O spare *him*, that *he* may recover strength, before *he* go hence, and be no more.

Above all, grant that this sudden visitation may be overruled for *his* everlasting welfare. May it humble *him* under the mighty hand of God. May it lead *him* to exercise true repentance towards Thee and unfeigned faith in the Lord Jesus Christ; and by Thy grace to cherish in *his* heart so deep a concern for the welfare of *his* soul, as no temptations shall be able to overcome. May *he* think upon *his* ways, and turn *his* feet unto Thy testimonies, and make haste to keep Thy commandments.

If it be Thy will that, in answer to our prayers, *he* should be yet spared in the land of the living, grant that *he* may, by Thy grace, be enabled to serve Thee more faithfully. But if it seem good to Thee to cut *him* off in the midst of *his* days, enable *him* meekly to bow to Thy holy will, and to depart in full assurance of faith. And grant *him*, through the merits and grace of the Redeemer, a portion in the inheritance of the saints.

Mercifully hear us, and grant an answer in peace, for the sake of Thy beloved Son, our Lord and Saviour. —*Amen.*

V.

PRAYER FOR A WOMAN IN TRAVAIL.

O GOD, the help of all that put their trust in Thee, be very merciful to Thine handmaid, for whom in her hour of travail we intercede.

Be not Thou far from her, O Lord, when trouble is nigh. Mitigate her sufferings. Relieve her anxieties. Give her grace to resign herself to Thy disposal, and patiently to submit to Thy most blessed will. Grant her a timely and safe deliverance from her pains and perils. And make her to be the thankful mother of a living infant, so that she may remember no more her anguish, for joy that a child is born into the world.

Above all, grant that her soul may prosper. Bestow on her for Christ's sake the pardon of all her sins. Enrich her with Thy loving-kindness, which is better than life. Increase her faith in Thy beloved Son, who is able to save unto the uttermost all who come unto Thee through Him. Sanctify her by the grace of Thy Holy Spirit, and make her meet to be a partaker of the inheritance of the saints in light. Cause Thy goodness and mercy to follow her all the days of her life; and receive her at last into those blessed mansions, which Thou hast prepared for them that love Thee; through Jesus Christ our Lord.—*Amen.*

VI.

THANKSGIVING FOR DELIVERANCE IN TRAVAIL.

FATHER of mercies, we give Thee thanks for Thy great goodness to Thy servant in her time of travail. Blessed be Thy name, that it hath pleased Thee to regard the low estate of Thine handmaid, and to grant her deliverance from the pains and perils of childbirth.

Continue Thy goodness by perfecting her recovery. Speedily restore her to health and strength. And grant that she may retain upon her mind a lively and lasting impression of Thy mercies; and that she may faithfully remember and pay to Thee the vows which she made to Thee when she was in trouble.

We praise Thee, O God, for the life which hath been spared, and also for the life which hath been given; and we pray that both may be precious in Thy sight, sustained by Thy care, and devoted to Thy glory. Preserve the new-born child, and train it for Thy service. Cause it to grow in grace as it grows in years. And grant that both mother and child may be so enabled to love, and honour, and serve Thee in this life, that they may finally meet in the enjoyment of everlasting glory and blessedness in the life to come, through Jesus Christ our Lord.—*Amen.*

VII.

FOR ONE WHO IS INSENSIBLE OR DELIRIOUS.

LORD GOD, merciful and gracious, who knowest our frame, and hast compassion on our infirmities, look down in pity, we beseech Thee, on Thy servant, for whom, in *his* present sorely afflicted state of body and of mind, we desire to intercede.

We earnestly pray, O God, that it may please Thee to enlighten *his* darkness, and to restore to *him* the use of all *his* faculties, that *he* may be able clearly to discern the things which belong to *his* everlasting peace. Arrest, if it be Thy will, the progress of *his* disease. Bless the means employed for its removal. Work for *him* a great deliverance for Thy mercy's sake; that, being restored to health of body and soundness of mind, *he* may be yet spared to serve Thee in the land of the living.

Above all, we entreat Thee to be merciful to *his* soul. Remember not against *him* former transgressions; remember Thy loving-kindnesses, which have been of old; and for the sake of Thy beloved Son, who bore our sins in His own body on the cross, receive *him* graciously, love *him* freely, and visit *him* with Thy salvation.

If it seem good to Thee in *his* present state to remove *him* from us, receive *him*, O Lord, unto Thyself, and in mercy give *him*, for Christ's sake, an entrance into Thy glorious kingdom, where all these dark shadows that now obscure *him* shall be removed, and in Thy light *he* shall see light.

Mercifully hear our humble supplications, for the Lord Jesus' sake.—*Amen.*

VIII.

FOR A SICK PERSON IN DEEP DEJECTION OF SPIRIT.

FATHER of mercies and God of all comfort, we pray that this, our *brother*, who is tempted by fear and doubt, may be cheered with the light of Thy reconciled countenance, and blessed with the consolations of Thy grace.

O Lord, rebuke *him* not in Thine anger, neither chasten *him* in Thy hot displeasure. Have mercy on *him*, for *he* is weak; heal *him*, for *his* soul is sore vexed. The troubles of *his* heart are enlarged; O bring Thou *him* out of *his* distresses. Look upon *his* affliction and *his* pain, and forgive all *his* sin. Let not the thought of Thy wrath lie hard upon *him*, nor the terror of Thy judgments distract or overwhelm *him*. Let *him* not doubt the truth of Thy promises, so graciously made in Thy beloved Son. Cause *him* to hear the voice of the Redeemer, inviting weary souls to come to Him and rest; assuring *him* that in no wise shall *he* be cast out. And let Thy Spirit work in *him* a lively faith, so that *he* may be filled with all joy and peace in believing, and may abound in hope through the power of the Holy Ghost.

Merciful Father, who hast comforted us with the assurance that Thou dost not afflict willingly nor grieve the children of men, suffer not our sorrowing *brother*, we beseech Thee, to think that Thou hast forgotten to be gracious to *him* by reason of these trials. Trusting in Thee as a reconciled God, may *he* be persuaded that in faithfulness Thou art chastening *him*, not for Thy pleasure, but for *his* profit. And having Thy love shed abroad within *his* heart, may *he* know that all things work together for *his* good, and that *his* present light affliction, which is but for a moment, worketh for *him* a far more exceeding, even an eternal weight of glory.

Grant, O God, if it be consistent with Thy holy will, that the malady of Thy servant may be removed, and that *he* may be spared to serve Thee on the earth. But if Thou shouldst have otherwise appointed, give *him* Thy grace to uphold *him* in a dying hour, that when *he* walks through the valley of the shadow of death *he* may fear no evil, because Thou, O Lord, art with *him*, and Thy rod and staff comfort *him*.

Grant these requests, O Father, in *his* behalf, and all other things which Thou knowest to be expedient for *him*, for the Lord Jesus' sake.—*Amen.*

IX.

FOR A SICK PERSON WHEN THERE IS LITTLE HOPE OF RECOVERY.

O GOD, in whose hand is the life of all mankind and the breath of every living thing, look with compassion on this Thy sorely afflicted servant, for whom we humbly offer our prayers.

Thou hast been pleased in Thy providence to bring *him* very low, and near to the gates of death: be pleased, therefore, we pray Thee, to give *him* Thy grace. Sustain *his* sinking heart, and give to *him* in rich measure the consolations of the Gospel.

Let Thy Holy Spirit be shed on *him* abundantly, to strengthen *him* for the endurance of *his* sufferings, to witness with *his* spirit that *he* is a child of God, to purify *him* from all remaining sin, and to make *him* meet for the inheritance of the saints in light.

God of all grace, support *him* in *his* time of trouble, that *his* faith be not shaken, nor *his* hope clouded, nor *his* peace disquieted by the trials that encompass *him*. Into Thy hands may *he* be enabled to commend *his* spirit, knowing whom *he* hath believed, and being persuaded that Thou art able to keep that which is committed to Thee against the great day. And if it be Thy will at this time to remove *him* from this world, grant *him* a peaceful departure out of this life, and graciously receive *him* to Thyself. Living or dying, O God, may *he* be Thine, safe in Thy hands and acceptable in Thy sight.

Comfort *his* anxious relatives and friends. Enable them to cast their care on Thee. Teach them to submit with meekness to Thy holy will, and give them grace to improve Thy chastening to the everlasting welfare of their souls.

These things we ask of Thee, O neavenly Father, only for the sake of Jesus Christ, Thy Son, our Saviour. —*Amen.*

X.

FOR ONE AT THE POINT OF DEATH.

O GOD, Father of mercies, and God of all consolation, look graciously, we beseech Thee, for Jesus Christ's sake, upon this Thy servant about to depart from this sinful world. Visit *him* with Thy salvation, and through the suffering and death of Christ Thy Son, mercifully grant *him* pardon and remission of all sin, that *he* in the hour of departure may find Thee a pitying Father; and, cleansed from all sin by the blood of Christ, may pass into life eternal, and into peace and the heavenly glory.

O Lord, in Thy mercy grant that *he* may know Thee to be *his* reconciled God; that *he* may be sensible in spirit of the presence of Christ with *him*, and that the light of the Holy Spirit may enlighten *him* in the dark hour of death.

O Lord, in Thy mercy comfort, sustain, guide, and bless for evermore this our departing friend, for whom Christ has died. Into Thy hands we commend *his* spirit. O our God, keep *him* safe for evermore.—*Amen.*

www.ingramcontent.com/pod-product-compliance
Lightning Source LLC
Chambersburg PA
CBHW020259170426
43202CB00008B/441